Counter-Cosmos
The Mind of the Mystic

Counter-Cosmos
The Mind of the Mystic

Dick Sullivan

Coracle Books

By the same author:

Prose
Old ships
Navvyman
Undertones: Mild Mysticism in an Age of Umber

Poetry
Capperbar
Melanie
The Moon at Midnight
Morning on the Mountain

ISBN 978 0 906280 88 1

For Mary

What is this cavern,
Cosmos-big but of no stone,
Unbounded by the bone?

It is, I think you'll find,
A counter-cosmos of the mind.

Capperbar

Contents

Foreword

Mysticism has been around for at least three thousand years – perhaps even longer: the Stone Age cave paintings in France and Spain were, I strongly suspect, in some ways mystical. It's one of the few things about us that hasn't changed, although today in the West it's faded away almost to nothing. But we've evolved culturally, not biologically, and the mystic instinct must still be buried there somewhere.

Mysticism is paradoxical at all levels. It's simple and at the same time impossible to understand. The first half of this book explains what mysticism is and why it's important. What good is it? What's it for? What does it feel like? What causes it? What kinds are there? Who has it?

The second half tries to show what low level mysticism can mean in daily life. Because no coherent argument can be made, it's set out after the manner of blog posts, looking at the theme from different angles. (By a mystic, I should add, I mean anybody who's had at least one spiritual experience – however minor – and acted on it in some way: many people have them and don't.)

Although mysticism is old, it's only in the last twenty or thirty years that it's become part (but only a part) of an academic discipline called Transpersonal Psychology. However, in both *Counter-Cosmos* and in it forerunner, *Undertones*, I've leaned heavily on a very few pre-Transpersonal authors. William James was an American psychologist and Pragmatist philosopher who, at the end of the Victorian era, made the first ever scientific study of mysticism. Evelyn Underhill was a mystic who wrote two good books about the subject. Caroline Spurgeon was a Professor of English in Bedford College, London, and the author of a book about writers who were also mystics. In his old age, Walter Terence Stace, one time Professor of Philosophy at Princeton, wrote two of the best books we have on mysticism. Alister Hardy was a zoologist who had mystic experiences in

9

childhood. When he retired in the 1960s he set up a research unit to study the spiritual. Aldous Huxley, the novelist (*Brave New World*), collected enough quotations to give us a global overview of what he, following Leibniz, called the *perennial philosophy*. William Ralph Inge was an Anglican clergyman whose lectures on mysticism are still essential reading. Finally there's Marghanita Laski, journalist, novelist and broadcaster, who conducted her own amateur survey in the 1950s. Of the eight, only Hardy and Underhill were mystics. Laski was an outright atheist while Inge was the only professional Christian. (Apart from Laski, all were Victorians as well.) (Potted biographies can be read in in the Appendix.)

Why these writers? I imagine you could put together quite a big dictionary of all the names coined for, and around, the mystic experience. An immense time span and geographical spread means that whole cultures and zeitgeists have come and gone, leaving behind encounters with mysticism in outdated language and outmoded ways of thought. The authors I've chosen put things over in language we can understand – Stace, for instance, seemed to regard the mystic moment as a meeting with pure Consciousness, a modern idea which means something to us immediately.

Laski, I suspect, is not even required reading on any Transpersonal psychology course. All the same, she was an intellectual who was well-read in literature but, because she knew little of the history of mysticism, had some fresh ideas about it. Stace brought the view point of a professional philosopher (an empiricist) to a subject of which he had no personal experience. Inge, also, was an educated Victorian with a learned Victorian's knowledge of church history and Greek philosophy. This mixture could hardly be repeated today, and certainly hasn't been.

Dick Sullivan
May 2011

Part One

Inge wrote: 'We live in two worlds which are so far related to each other that if we deny all reality to either of them, the other fades away.' Without the spiritual, in other words, societies decay. But mysticism is the essence of the spiritual. If Inge is right, therefore, it's of the greatest importance. So what is it? Who has it? What causes it? What is it not?

CHAPTER ONE:

The Well-Lived Day

What is mysticism *for*? Einstein – who *was* a mystic – said it's the seed of all art, science, culture and religion. 'The most beautiful emotion we can experience... the sower of all true art and science.' Without it you're as good as dead. It tells us that God is really there, really does exist. It shows itself through wisdom and beauty although we're too primitive to see it properly. Scientists, theoretical physicists in particular, are more prone than anybody else to mystical experiences, or so thought Einstein. And, strangely enough, C P 'Two Cultures' Snow said something similar but from a different angle: 'the feelings aroused by scientific knowledge are the same as the feelings known to religious mystics'. Without it, people aren't wholly alive.

Stace, who was not a mystic himself, thought mystics were on to something. Even if it's a deluded illusion, it still reveals something 'supremely great in human life – 'the peace which passeth all understanding'. It's the gateway to salvation – not in a future life but as the highest beatitude that a man can reach in this life, and out of which the greatest deeds of love can flow.'

Marghanita Laski was an atheist who never accepted there was anything supernatural about mystic experiences (nor did she have them herself). But ecstasies, as she called them, are good for you physically and mentally. They boost creativity and make the mind more complex. What's a good touchstone for proving the genuineness of an ecstatic moment? Out of her long list, the best is probably what she called 'the test of benefit'. She quoted St Teresa of Avila: if the experience makes you bigger and better you can take it that it's the real thing.

Laski also speculated that inspiration was the lowest rung of the mystic ladder. Blake had no doubt about it: 'One thing alone makes a poet – Inspiration, the divine vision'. More exactly he called it the Three-Fold Vision which looks through base matter to Eternity beyond. Another unknown man – a writer perhaps in the Hampstead Hills – told Laski, rather nicely, that inspiration makes for a 'well-lived day'. Not quite Einstein's endorsement but worth having any way.

Jung, who had at least one major mystic experience, thought that a meeting with the spiritual was necessary to cure neuroses as well as for individuation. Most of his middle-aged patients were, in fact, really only looking for the spiritual. To be healed, they needed the numinous. Individuation means becoming fully human, becoming what you're born to be. Nobody is born to be empty and, for some, the spiritual is the final in-filler.

Inge, being a churchman, thought mysticism is the raw material of religion and art. 'Formless and vague or fleeting as it is, mystical experience is the bedrock of religious faith. In it the soul, acting as a unity with all faculties, rises above itself and becomes a spirit, it asserts its claim to be a citizen of heaven.' It's the raw stock of art, and art is an opening into the spiritual.

At the end of his study of mysticism, William James summed up what he'd found: it confers a 'new zest which adds itself like a gift to life, and takes the form either of lyrical enchantment or an appeal to earnestness and heroism. An assurance of safety and a temper of peace, and, in relation to others, a preponderance of loving affections'.

Alister Hardy said it gives us a 'sense of joy, peace, security, awe, reverence, and wonder; feelings of exaltation and ecstasy, of harmony and unity, of hope and fulfilment'. And, if that isn't enough, he added a sense of 'timelessness .. of presence .. of purpose .. of prayer answered in events.'

In the late 1950s, a man wrote to Marghanita Laski about his experiences. He was a middle-aged newspaper packer who'd left school at fifteen around the time of the Great War. The mystic experience wasn't ordinary happiness, he told her. It was brought on by 'sunsets, beautiful music, scenery from heights, eg from Snowdon, Helvellyn, etc. Also masses of flowers.' It had occurred dozens of times to him and was 'indescribable. Peace, accompanied by a little heavier breathing and sometimes a feeling of wanting to close my eyes and cry'. As for changing him he said: 'Not exactly changed but certainly strengthened my appreciation of life'. He'd never read a book about mysticism and gave as his religion 'Rationalist'.

Others pitched the odds even higher, claiming that the fate of the West rested on a re-spiritualising of society. Ruskin called the nineteenth century the Age of Umber and thought the darkness of the times was caused by a lack of faith. Where the Greeks saw gods in the woods, Victorians saw poachers. He also said that landscape itself can give you a sense of sanctity and that all beautiful things can, in some mystic way, lead to a meeting with the Divine. Art tells us the truth about religion (because art is spiritual) and about the way we should live: it's the embodiment of a civilisation, revealing how great or how rotten it is. The Middle Ages got the connection between life, work and art just about right and had therefore created a spiritual wholeness. Modern art is a kind of anxiety and art is failing because it's removed from its sacred roots.

Huxley, who was no mystic (though he wanted to be one), said you can judge the quality of a society by how it helps people grow 'towards the goal of human existence' – which is, quite simply, a meeting with the divine. But, in spite of its importance, the West had turned away from the spiritual, towards the material. Writing in 1946, he also stressed what happened without it – nationalism, statism, revolutionism and 'state-worship, boss-worship'. The cause of the decline, Huxley thought, was Christianity's homing in too hard on history – what happened in Galilee and Judea in the 1st century – and an 'undervaluation of the everlasting, timeless fact of eternity'.

In the 1960s, Alister Hardy set up his Religious Experience Research Unit to collect and sift through mystical experiences, rather after the manner of William James (and Edwin Starbuck and James Leuba). This was because he was a man with an agenda: the West was in decay from the lack of a spiritual dimension and he hoped to find a way to reverse it. The spiritual is normal and necessary but the natural craving for it was being blocked and frustrated by materialism. That 'unappeased religious desire' needed the support of a spiritual philosophy which, in turn, doesn't contradict science and the Theory of Evolution. He wanted Extra-Sensory Perception (ESP) to be a fact because it would make a spiritual dimension more plausible. (He carried out experiments himself, unsuccessfully. A few years later, Rhine's original tests in Duke University were also shown to be flawed.)

Speaking in 1899, Inge said: 'when the free current of the religious life is dammed up ... it turns into a swamp, and poisons human society'. He went on: 'The constructive task which lies before the (20th century) is to spiritualise science, as morality and art have already been spiritualised.' Like amphibians, we live in two worlds – in our case, the material and the spiritual. Both must be in balance. If one decays, the other can't flourish and will also fade away.

CHAPTER TWO

What Is It? Who Has It?

Two things about mysticism can't be denied. First, it happens when the mind has briefly shut down and thinking has stopped. Secondly, it's a factual experience which can change people for the better. At its most intense, mysticism feels like a dissolving of the self into 'the unity underlying diversity', as Caroline Spurgeon put it. But what is it that the extreme mystic merges with? For science-approving Westerners the least arguable answer is Consciousness.

'A different kind of consciousness,' Stace called it. It's different because it's void of all thought, feeling, emotion, ideas or concepts. It can't include any of these (at the highest level at least) because it's a single unbroken entity with no room for anything but pure consciousness, conscious only of itself. It's complete and indivisible. Don't try thinking about it because reason can't reach it. You can experience it, that's all.

Is that so strange? Can anything be stranger than the fact of consciousness itself ? How matter can generate non-matter is one of the great unresolved riddles of science. In his book, *The Spiritual Nature of Man,* Hardy notes that as far back as 1915, Emile Durkheim was talking about a 'collective consciousness' as the 'highest form of psychic life'. Most importantly, the collective consciousness is outside us and so 'sees things only in their permanent and essential aspects'. Sir Charles Sherrington thought of the brain as 'an organ of liaison between energy and mind', not as 'a converter of energy into mind or *vice versa'.* I'm not sure science even now has anything more profound to say about consciousness, or thought.

16

Nor need the 21st century West automatically think of mysticism as being 'supernatural'. Hardy, for example, shied away from that word, choosing 'paraphysical' instead. To him, the apparently para-normal is normal.

Having said all that, most people *do* think of mysticism as supernatural or religious which, in the West, usually means Christianity. Yet mysticism and a Creator God don't fit together at all well. This is probably because exoteric theologians see Twoness (Creator/creature) where esoteric mystics see Oneness. The best solution came out of 14th century Germany, from the man Stace called 'the most profoundly philosophical, original, and independent of all the Christian mystics'. He was Eckhart von Hochheim, more commonly known as Meister Eckhart, a German, a Dominican friar, a one-time student in Paris, one-time professor in Strasbourg, twice a Vicar-General (Saxony and Bohemia) and a preacher who pulled in the crowds.

What the mystic sees, Eckhart said, goes deeper than the Trinity to what he called the Godhead (or Godhood – Godness Itself). Only a small part of a human being can experience this depth of spirituality. He called that part the 'apex of the soul' or the 'spark'. 'Diess fuenkelein, das ist Gott.' 'This spark is God'. Quite literally. The apex of the spirit sees the Infinite because it is itself infinite, sees the Godhead because it too is, literally, the Godhead. The soul's apex and the Trinity are both off-shoots of the Godhead which alone is prior and prime. Today, we might say that the Trinity is an over-belief. But the underlying unity is not a belief at all – it's an experience. Whether or not it genuinely comes from something outside the mind, of course, is impossible to say. But given the oddity of consciousness in the first place, I'm not sure it matters very much.

Yet it doesn't quite end there. We're dealing with a spectrum, a sliding scale of intensity, and this kind of 'union-with-divinity' takes place only at its extreme end. In the surveys he undertook in the 1970s, Hardy wanted to separate 'a general sense of spiritual awareness' from those experiences of 'a more dramatic, mystical character'. He called these experiences the *mystical* and the *numinous.* The *mystical* is a 'feeling of the merging of the self with a divine reality'. The *numinous* – following Rudolf Otto who coined the word – is 'an awareness of the holy'. John Polkinghorne, a quantum physicist *and* an Anglican priest, also used mystical and numinous but added a phrase – *effect of prayer and/or worship* – to describe a third mystic level.

A simpler way is to think of three broad bands of mysticism major, minor and *undertones.* Undertones are, I suspect, what Polkinghorne means by the *effect of prayer* and what Hardy meant by *awareness of the holy.* Laski called them *adamic* experiences after Adam and Eve – a vision of the Garden of Eden in all its purity, innocence and kindness. Undertones/ adamic events are different in degree, but not in kind, from the higher forms of mysticism. They are less intense and most likely to be daily. If full blown mysticism is a blaze, mild mysticism is torchlight and an undertone is a spark.

An analogy – suggested by Huxley – might help. Many words in English should be synonyms because they have the same root-meanings in different languages: 'maternal' and 'motherly', for example, or 'feminine' and 'womanly'. What gives them very different meanings are the overtones they carry. Undertones are spiritual overtones. They appear when the opaque solidity of the world is stretched to translucence to let a blurred soft light shine through. Or they're like peripheral sight: something's there but can't say what and when you turn your head it moves too. We struggle to describe them because the self, which normally stands aside to watch and take note, is no longer there. By definition, the mystic moments comes when the ego has collapsed, leaving a vacuum to be filled by an all-pervading, impersonal Benignity. (Even undertones, of course, have different degrees of intensity.)

Only one or two more points need adding. Mystic experiences can be either inner or outer or, as Stace put it, 'extrovertive or introvertive'. In other words, they are caused either by something in the world outside the mind or by the mind's turning inwards and closing itself down from within. Probably the inner is the more major and, more often than not, is deliberately sought via mind-stopping exercises.

There are, in fact, two broad ways to get there, introvertively speaking: contemplation and meditation. Contemplation is mind stilling via any one of dozens of different ways: yoga, zazen, the Jesus Prayer, mantras, yantras, tantras, kundalini, transcendental meditation, the drumming of Siberian shamans. Counting your breathing in and out is a common way also.

Meditation usually means staring at something – a mandala, crucifix, leaf or almost anything else: what, doesn't really matter. St Teresa of Avila said to her nuns: 'I do not require of you to form great and curious considerations in your understanding: I require of you no more than to *look*'. And concentrate, she might have added: concentrate until the mind's swirling stops.

Extrovertive experiences, which as we've seen are triggered by something outside the mind, are more usually spontaneous. At the high end of the extrovertive scale, these events transfigure the things of the world and at the same time show them to be a single entity. Although Stace doesn't quote him, Thomas Traherne illustrates what he seems to have had in mind. 'The dust and stones of the street were as precious as gold?.... Boys and girls tumbling in the street were moving jewels?... The city seemed to stand in Eden, or to be built in Heaven.' At the lower end of the scale, however, these extrovertive experiences are mild adamic undertones which briefly displace the self, leaving a gap which is instantly filled by an upwelling of benignity.

Counter-Cosmos, it can now be said, is primarily about extrovertively-triggered adamic experiences.

And what of degrees of mysticism? If we make a (guess-work) Mystic Scale from 0 to 100, somebody like the Buddha and perhaps St Teresa of Avila get the top mark: Eckhart (I'd guess) comes in around 95, Wordsworth 60, other even more minor mystics 45-60, those at the undertone level 25 to 45.

Then there's the big question of: 'who?' Who has these experiences and what percentage of the population have them? John of Ruysbroeck, a Fleming, was one of the greatest of the 14th century Eckhartian school of mystics. He'd been brought up by two monks, one of whom was probably his uncle. Until the age of fifty he served as a jobbing priest in the Cathedral in Brussels. Then, for the last thirty-eight years of his life, he lived and worked in a forest twenty or so miles from the city. To him, the spiritual life is a progressive pilgrimage: it's all about growth, a journey to the mystic meeting place where 'you'll abide inwardly in unbroken repose'. (But not idly – you're not supposed to bask in your good fortune but get out there and help others, or climb back down the ladder as he put it.)

Religious people, he thought, fall into four types. Unmystical *Hirelings* are in it only for themselves, and are therefore spiritually impoverished. *Marthas* have no mystic interiors either but are faithful to outward rituals and exoteric beliefs. Third are the *Secret Friends* who, if I understand him correctly, have mystical leanings but blight them, or can't take them forward. More realistically, perhaps, they are minor mystics, open to mild ecstatic experiences or a lifetime of undertones. The fourth kind Ruysbroeck called the *God Seeing,* clearly the major kind of mystic such as himself and Eckhart.

And percentages? Here we're much less sure. I'm familiar with only two surveys, both now old. (Transpersonal psychologists may have done more.) Laski carried out a private one, mainly among her friends and neighbours, in the 1950s. Ten years later Alister Hardy set up his Religious Experience Unit in Oxford.

Laski's first sample was very small: sixty-three adults. It has to be stressed that they lived in the Hampstead Hills, one of London's richest areas. She was a professional writer and TV personality and nearly a third of her first sample were professional authors also. Almost all the rest were from a similar background. Of the sixty-three all but two had experienced 'transcendent ecstasy'. That's around ninety-seven percent – an enormously high figure. Can it possibly be right?

Some time later, she posted a hundred copies of a doctored version of the questionnaire ('transcendent' became 'unearthly') through letter boxes in a 'working class district of London'. A stamped addressed envelope was enclosed but no cash incentive. She was lucky to get eleven replies, particularly as ten of them said 'no'. Only one said 'yes' – the newspaper packer we've already met. One percent versus ninety-seven? Can that be right?

She also sent her questionnaire to fifteen-year old girls in a Grammar School. None had had any ecstatic experiences. Again that must be doubtful. Fifteen percent of the four thousand people who wrote in to Hardy's research unit in the 1970s thought their childhood experiences of the transcendent were of lifelong importance.

More realistically, surveys carried out by the National Opinion Poll on behalf of two of Hardy's assistants showed that forty-one percent of females and thirty-one percent of males had had mystical experiences. A substantial minority of that order feels about right, although we can't be too sure since Hardy included accounts in his survey which seem to be far from mystical. (Maslow, too, I think, confused euphoria with Laskian ecstasies.)

In the end, although with such a little to go on, Laski concluded, very tentatively, that the ecstatic experience was reserved for 'creatives', 'intellectuals' and the educated, certainly at the higher levels. Working people and children, she decided, were probably capable only of mysticism's lower slopes. This however overlooks the fact that the girls were in a Grammar School which, in those days, meant they were above average intelligence. She also overlooked the fact that many working class people back then had been handicapped by birth and a lack of opportunity, not an absence of brains or creativity. Educated people, too, might be better at putting into words what has happened to them and are also more likely to be heard if they do speak up.

One final curiosity: Laski didn't baulk at Evelyn Underhill's rather farfetched idea that the mystically inclined are more highly evolved and are, in fact, the vanguard of what mankind will become. (Sri Aurobindo had a similar idea, I believe: he thought a new 'supra-mental' being was evolving.) But all of that, I think, we can shelve.

CHAPTER THREE

Triggers and Switches

One thing and one thing only is the cause of mysticism – the shutting down of the mind. It's as simple (and as hard) as that. But although there is no other way, there are different routes. Meditation and contemplation are the introvertive ones. Extrovertively, we usually have to rely on something in the outside world triggering a shut-down. (As far as I know, Laski was the first to use the word 'trigger' in this sense. 'Switch' would do just as well.) In his book, *The Spiritual Nature of Man,* Hardy lists eighteen triggers or switches:

'Depression/despair' unexpectedly take the top place. The rest, in descending order, are: prayer/meditation, natural beauty, worship, literature/films, illness, music, crises in personal relations, death of others, sacred places, visual art, creative work, relaxation, silence/solitude *and* (jointly at 14) the prospect of death, physical activity, childbirth, happiness, physical love. The Number 1 slot had 183.7 mentions out of a thousand. No 18 had only 4.

There are of course many others. A sense of continuity through time can be one. Jacquetta Hawkes advises you to look at your hand and 'feel its bones and nails' and then try to visualise 'dark, warm mud squeezing between scaly claws.' She was a mystic as well as an archaeologist, a rare combination, you'd imagine. Her book, *A Land,* written in the 1940s when she was in her own thirties, is about the living presence of the deep past in the present. In it she traces the history of England from the laying down of the rocks to the coming of people and what they did to the landscape. It's also a mysticism of place and its poetry. 'Hardy's poems grew from the Wessex downlands, Clare's from the tiny stretch of the Midlands in which alone he felt at home;

Crabbe's are the bitter fruit of the Norfolk (*sic*) Coast: 'There poppies, nodding mock the hope of toil,/There the blue bugloss paints the sterile soil."

Archaeologists might well be moved by the past but Jung's (one and only?) mystical experience was also triggered by deep prehistory. 'Standing on a little hill in the East African plains, I saw herds of thousands of wild beasts, grazing in soundless peace, beneath the breath of the primaeval world, as they had done for unimaginable ages of time, and I had the feeling of being the first man, the first being to know that all this *is*. The whole world around me was still in the primitive silence and knew not what it was. In this very moment in which I knew it the world came into existence, and without this moment it would never have been.'

Landscape can, clearly, be a switch. Some years ago I was working on a documentary about microscopes. One was the portable MacArthur (invented by John MacArthur in a Japanese prison camp during the War). To demonstrate how it worked we filmed a freshwater biologist examining algae in the falls which flow into Derwentwater behind the Swiss Chalet Hotel near Kendal. The crew were filming her. My next job was the on-camera interview and so I was standing apart, higher up in the woods, thinking about the questions.

All at once I felt myself slipping into the landscape, sinking, becoming part of it. Not a separate part because no parts were separate: all was one partless whole. It must have lasted a few seconds only before I struggled to get out of it, something I regretted at the time. Why did I do that? The thinking mind beat the non-thinking one, I suspect. Also I was not alone and had a job to do. It was much deeper than the common or garden undertone: up to sixty on the mystic scale, maybe. It was also, of course, extrovertive.

Inge has quite a few new and original things to say about nature mysticism. He begins by pointing out that the Church Fathers stressed the beauty of nature but disparaged art. He mentions the mysticism of St Francis of Assissi and the reverence for nature found in Renaissance Platonists like Plutarch, Bruno and Campanella. But nature mysticism, he points out, is not the same as seeing God's hand in natural things. It's what happens when something in nature stops you thinking. In English at least, Inge thought that 'the greatest Prophet of this branch of contemplative Mysticism is unquestionably the poet Wordsworth.' Wordsworth was a natural born Platonist who found his philosophy of life early and lived by it (except, of course, he lost his sensitivity to the mystical in his mid-thirties).

Inge seems to have thought that this extrovertive kind of nature mysticism was Post-Reformation. Not really. The 13th century Spanish missionary, Ramon Lull, was also a nature mystic. Nor was it purely a Protestant thing: two 16th century Spanish Catholics – Luis de Granada and Luis de Leon (both of whom were hounded by the Inquisition) – were nature mystics and poets. The Luis from Granada wrote not only of the usual things – sea shells and the night sky – but also the spawning of fish and frogs. In England, too, nature mysticism didn't begin with the Romantics: Henry Vaughan has a claim to being an early example and although Gray wasn't a mystic himself his *Elegy* is crammed with extrovertive undertones:

> Now fades the glimmering landscape on the sight,
> And all the air a solemn stillness holds,
> Save where the beetle wheels his droning flight,
> And drowsy tinklings lull the distant folds.

And also, of course, people lived with nature long before they were urbanised: nature mysticism must therefore be as old as the hills. There is, for example, a strong strain of it in Japanese literature: the original impulse behind haiku was pure nature mysticism, I suspect.

Motion is another, rather off-beat, trigger which Laski identified. Walking, we know, releases an endorphin to bring on a small bout of happiness. Laski goes further: motion can trigger an ecstatic event. To prove it, she quotes the fact that Wordsworth wrote *Westminster Bridge* on top of a coach. He seems to have written at least three other poems – all unmemorable – in the same place. Their unmemorability does suggest, on the other hand, that the coach ride wasn't all that ecstatic. Most of Wordsworth's real work, of course, *was* written

24

while in motion – walking on the Lakeland fells.

All that's well known. What isn't is the mystic boyhood of Roger Bannister, the first man to run a four minute mile. In his autobiography he tells of becoming aware, while running one morning on the sea shore, that 'each of the myriad particles of sand was perfect in its way'. As he ran he 'discovered a new unity with nature'.

I can also partly vouch for the power of motion since, as a seventeen year old, I spent one afternoon a week on a cross-country run. It wasn't a race, so you could run alone, down into a valley and through open country along the banks of a river. In Laski's terms, I suppose the experience was – or could be described as – mildly adamic. It was a wintertime run but November was best – still dripping and misty and the ground not frost-solid as it became in January in the harder climate back then.

Then, of course, there's beauty. Hardy's list, I think, is a bit suspect in this area: even if you add together all his triggers which involve beauty, they don't amount to a lot. Yet beauty is probably the biggest switch of them all, in spite of the fact that Plotinus said it takes you only half way to the Divine: to get the rest of the way, you need to 'love the Good' (or God). The Plotinian message is: don't get bogged down in beauty which is only like the booster of a two-stage rocket. Ruskin disagreed. To him, beauty is not an ante-chamber to God, it is God Himself.

Mallarmé, the French Symbolist poet, may also have thought that Beauty and the Ultimate were the same thing. Not God, however: he was an atheist who was equally against religion and science since neither led to the truth. His symbols were supposed to by-pass what Robert Graves called 'prose meaning' and deliver you straight to the mystic meeting point. Baudelaire had a similar idea: the artist's job is to 'clarify and express the consciousness which acts within the material world, but at the same time transcends time and space'. Mind you, he was into hashish and the occult which, as we'll see, are mystically suspect.

Mysticism goes back a long way, if not perhaps quite as far as the hominids. Certainly it stretches back to the Axial Age – mankind's pivot – between 700 and 200 BC. What things were like before then we can't really know. Huxley points out that mysticism hasn't changed since then, which either means it taps into a deep unchangingness at the heart of things or that neurophysiological evolution has stalled. Probably the latter. All the same, in the 1950s Laski put names to aspects of mysticism which must have always been known, if nameless. Response, Revelation and Desolation ecstasies are three of them.

Some places are more likely than others to trigger a mystic event. A response experience occurs when you put yourself in a position where you can expect one to come along. In that regard, Laski also has something new to say about the poet Housman, a man who's puzzled me for some years. Nothing about him says mystic and yet so much of his poetry is undertone-invoking. On the other hand, Laski argues that Housman was a mild ecstatic. Her reason, not a strong one, is based on a well-known passage: 'Experience,' Housman wrote, 'has taught me, when I am shaving in the morning, to keep watch over my thoughts, because, if a line of poetry strays into my memory, my skin bristles so that the razor ceases to act. This particular symptom is accompanied by a shiver down the spine; there is another which consists in a constriction of the throat and a precipitation of water to the eyes; and there is a third which I can only describe by borrowing a phrase from one of Keats's last letters, where he says, speaking of Fanny Brawne, 'everything that reminds me of her goes through me like a spear'. The seat of this sensation is the pit of the stomach.'

Every afternoon after lunch in Cambridge, Housman took a stroll, alone, rudely speaking to nobody. Laski claims he was deliberately putting himself in a position where he could expect some kind of response experience. Lines, even whole stanzas certainly did crop up in his mind from time to time, along with a 'sudden and unaccountable emotion'. Except his poetry came in two main bursts twenty years apart and died out with the death of Moses Jackson, the man he unrequitedly loved. Perhaps, though, he was waiting for inspiration to un-do the corruption in the Latin texts which were his true life's work. Lull the mind and answers to problems do come along.

Laski certainly got one thing wrong. In *Ecstasy,* she says

patriotism has never acted as a trigger for an ecstatic experience. Quite a lot of Housman's poetry does – or did – do just that for a great many people. She's right, though, about response experiences – they're very real, particularly if you accept that inspiration is a mystic event. Even if you don't, you can't deny that it works, particularly for siphoning up words and phrases you would never otherwise have thought of. The trick is put yourself in a landscape, with pen and clipboard, empty the mind and let the words come. (Or not: it's outside conscious control.) Emptying the mind is the key thing, of course: but some landscapes are more conducive to that than others.

I'm less sure about what she called Revelation Experiences. She meant that some things, which begin as triggers, become ecstatically charged themselves. The trigger is no longer a means to an end, it's the end itself. What was previously just another mechanical way of stoppimg the workings of the mind, now has a value in its own right.

Here's a *possible* example of what I think she may have meant. One summer's day a long time ago I was on the banks of the River Test in Hampshire working on a film about waterweed. (Sodium alginate when dribbled into water turns into soluble strings. Mix it with Paraquat and you can draw lines of weed killer in the river.) A man fished under the shade of the trees. The sun shone. The river flowed on, dappled and sparkling although a little weed-bound in places.

The director was a painter and a bit of a mystic, as I found out later. It was our first job together and he was known to be awkward and quite liable to walk away from a shoot. It was therefore too fraught a day for undertones and, besides, you need to be alone for that. Being alone had to be wait until I came to write the commentary a few weeks later. What I came across was a Laskian Revelation Experience. Somehow, in those strips of 16mm Eastmancolour negative, the director had revealed another way of looking at water. Water for me then took on a strange new other-worldliness. Rivers and water – all water – had gained a deeper meaning. Like consciousness, there's an inexplicable strangeness about it which is unearthly. So why am I less sure about all of this? Adamic events are in the mind, not in matter – a revelation experience, I suspect, is just a very reliable trigger which works every time.

We're on firmer ground with Desolation Experiences which, although slightly strange, are still no more than straightforward triggers. Nor are they as bad as they sound because there has to be, I think, a metaphorical rope tethering you to safety for them to work properly. A fifteen year old school girl who replied to Laski's questionnaire gave a good example. The girl, then aged around ten, had been on holiday with her family near Ullswater. One day, she'd run far ahead of them, half lost in the rain and the bracken, on the high fells. 'I became aware of something .... Two enormous menacing peaks towered above me ... I felt I was being lifted from my feet.' She stepped closer to the edge of a crag and looked down into 'a huge pit of choppy black water.' She ran back to her family, still in the distance. It was a Desolation experience followed by a Revelation: 'I knew I could never really enjoy myself unless I was surrounded by hills, moors and crags, and the ancient Roman roads that ramble endlessly over them.'

The Torridon Mountains (to take an example at random) falling sheer, dark and menacing from black cloud cover to black sea can have that effect also. Most desolate places can – salt marshes at dusk, or the great sphagnum bog of Sutherland with the endless wind wuthering across it day and night. They seem to inspire a sense of something greater than your own small self and that, in turn, triggers a sensation of something greater still. The feeling induced by the peak which seemed to to follow and threaten Wordsworth as he rowed his borrowed boat one night on Windermere was also, perhaps, a desolation experience.

CHAPTER FOUR

What Mysticism is Not

Stace begins *The Teachings of the Mystics* by saying what mysticism is *not*. It's *not* 'misty, foggy, vague, or sloppy'. *Not* 'mystery-mongering.' *Not* 'the occult, spiritualism, ghosts or table turning'. It's not about 'telepathy, telekinesis, clairvoyance, precognition'.

Inge, who was an Anglican and no admirer of Rome, had his own list of what mysticism is not: it's not 'What the older Catholic writers call mystical phenomenon or supernatural favours – mysterious sights, sounds and smells, 'boisterous' fits of weeping, cataleptic trances, stigmata, apparitions and the like.'

Mediums are not mystics. It has nothing to do with ouija boards, crystals, astrology, horoscopes, tarot cards, palmistry, reading tea leaves, reading coffee grounds, reading entrails. It isn't ESP, levitation or anything New Age. Nor is it magic, ley lines, astral planes, wicca, witchcraft, faith healing, exorcism or casting spells. Speaking in tongues is unmystical and so is common or garden euphoria.

True mystics fall into two kinds, says Stace: the emotional and intellectual – foremost among the latter, in the West, being Eckhart who believed, understandably, that his type was superior to the emotional lot who were often unbalanced, not to say unhinged. Intellectual mystics are cool, serene and sane. Only the emotionals hear voices and see visions. Visions and voices, as Stace says (correctly), are unmystical. What happened to St Paul at Damascus therefore could be a myth – a story which is spiritually, but not factually, true – because elsewhere in the *Epistles* he clearly *is* a mystic.

William James may well have been echoing this divide when

29

he spoke about healthy-minded mystics and those who are sick in their souls. The sick of soul worry about wickedness and pain in a world made by a good God. But James's idea is a bit suspect – in the mystic state people are soul-whole, not soul-sick. He quotes Bunyan as a soul-sick example, but isn't *The Pilgrim's Progress* pure exoteric Puritanism? An allegory?

Raptures, trances, hyper-emotionalism are also unmystical, being, most probably, hysteria – St Teresa, for example, knew that *some* of her visions were hallucinations. With others it was all pure pretence. In 16th century Spain, a Franciscan nun (an Abbess, no less) called Magdalena de la Cruz fooled everybody into thinking she was a mystic. For thirty-eight years she faked terrifying visions and sported, but didn't fake, self-made stigmata. When she repented, after being very ill, she blamed it all on the Devil who'd told her to do it.

Some people think Blake was insane – Robert Graves did – and it's not hard to see why. This was the man who saw the ghost of his dead brother clapping his hands as he rose through the ceiling, who later spoke to St Joseph in person, who saw angels hanging like apples from trees, and who at the age of four saw God looking in at the window. Yet he was also, like St Teresa, a true mystic although, unlike her, he never saw through himself.

Among celibate monks and nuns some of the hysteria was almost certainly sexual. Suso, a monk of the Eckhartian school in the 14th century, is one of the very oddest. Dean Inge tells his story at some length. Suso lived most of his life by Lake Constance and called himself 'The Servitor of the Divine Wisdom'. Wisdom, a woman, ordered him to scourge and torture himself, which he did for sixteen years. He even cut the word 'Jesus' into his chest. Then he asked a passing angel to show him where God lived in his soul. Suso's flesh became clear as glass and he saw his own soul lying in the arms of Wisdom.

Another time the dead Eckhart visited to tell him that he, Eckhart, was now 'made God-like in God'. You too can become the same, Eckhart told him, by detaching yourself from the world and dying to self, as well as maintaining 'unruffled patience with all men'.

Oddest of all (for today if not the 14th century) was the time when the Virgin Mary came along with the infant Jesus. Suso asked her to 'show him the Child, and to suffer him also to kiss it. When she kindly offered it to him,' (Inge goes on, presumably paraphrasing Suso's autobiography), 'he spread out his arms and received the beloved One. He contemplated its beautiful little eyes, he kissed its tender little mouth, and he gazed again and again at all the infant members of the heavenly treasure. Then lifting up his eyes, he uttered a cry of amazement that he who bears the heaven is so great, and yet so small, so beautiful in heaven and so childlike on earth.'

Later, another angel told Suso he must become a knight, but he baulked at this and asked God if he hadn't suffered enough. No, said God: hitherto you've 'stricken' yourself but henceforth *I* am going to strike you: you'll lose your his good name, be treated treacherously, and in the end even I will forsake you. Not long after this, Suso was robbed and beaten by bandits. The chief thief had already drowned one priest in the Rhine – after confessing his sins to him. Worse, a prostitute claimed Suso had fathered her child. His superiors didn't believe her but he paid for the child's keep (with what?).

In his book, *Western Society and the Church in the Middle Ages,* R W Southern tells the story of the beguines of 13th century Cologne. It seems the Black Death left more women alive than men. Many women, with no hope of marriage, took an oath to live secular but religious lives in chastity. They worked in hospitals or as weavers and embroiderers. Southern refers to their 'ecstatic and visionary experiences with a strong element of naive sexuality in their imagery'. One of them, Mechthild of Magdeburg, is known today because of her book *Fliessende licht der Gottheit* ('Flowing light of the Godhead'). In one startling passage her senses tell her soul to imagine that it's suckling the infant Christ. 'I'm a woman and bride,' she tells her senses, 'and I want my Lover'. She writes of her soul being caressed while sitting in the lap of her lawful husband, God. Elsewhere her soul tells her body that she has no more use for it. 'My soul is in the highest bliss,/for she has seen/and thrown her arms around her Loved One all at once.'

Whatever all this was, it wasn't mystic. One the side of

common sense we have the 14th century English mystic, Walter Hilton, and St Albertus Magnus. Hilton said you can't trust visions because they could come from Satan. The only test – one we come across down the centuries – is 'does this make us bigger and better?'. If not, it's the Devil's work. Albertus Magnus, the 13th century Dominican friar who brought Aristotle into the church to balance its Platonism, tried to reconcile his own mystical experiences with Scholasticism. God, he argued, is a spirit and therefore the senses are of no use in finding Him. Only an undistracted descent through the darkness of the mind followed by an ascent into light can do that. If the senses are involved in any way at all you're on the wrong tack. Visions and voices, that is, are not mystical.

Likewise, euphoria and delusions are also unmystical, though many people confuse them with the real thing. Not everybody who wrote to Hardy's spiritual research unit in the 1970s had had true mystical experiences, I suspect. God told one elderly man to go to Nigeria and teach. A lot of the accounts Hardy collected are as unsubtle and specific as that: too self-centred or, better, centred unselfishly on the self. The point about mysticism is that 'me' is banished if not abolished.

Some accounts could be looked at in two different ways. A mother was kneeling by the coffin of her seven year old daughter. 'Then I felt a touch on my shoulder lasting only an instant, and I knew there was another world'. A soldier, about to go ashore at Gallipoli in 1915, felt a 'Presence' which turned his fear to ecstasy. Then he was shot and crippled. Grief and fear, I suppose, could have cut off thought and let something else break through. But it's not obvious that these examples are anything other than the mind finding non-mystical comfort in the face of overwhelming fear and grief.

Out-of-body experiences are doubtful too – 'lucid dreams' Hardy calls some of them, although he does go on to quote at length a rather beautiful account given him by an old lady who was then nearly a hundred. It had happened when she'd been a young mother, probably at the end of the Victorian era. She was on holiday one June with her two small children near the sea in Cornwall. Only one or two jarring notes (calling the children 'chicks' and 'tinies' grates a bit) spoil her nicely written story. She was a religious woman – her holiday reading was *The Prayer Book*, *The Bible* and Thomas à Kempis. At four o'clock one afternoon on the cliffs near Tintagel (King Arthur's Camelot?) the world was transformed. 'The old church behind us was, I saw, outlined by a stream of golden light. Looking inland, I saw every hedge giving off golden flames, quivering.' At first she'd thought that her eyes had been blinded by the sun path on the sea. 'Then I turned and saw my double, my body, getting up and busying herself with the children, putting them in their little push-chair'. (Strangely, she felt a touch of jealousy.)

The split lasted for the rest of the day: she watched her other 'she' having tea and talking to a Mrs B (the landlady?). In the evening, both went for stroll. The other-she, in the lead, clambered heavily over a stile which the out-of-body-she 'sailed' over. This was odd because the out-of-body-she felt herself to be solid also: that night, in fact, she may have written the account which, years later, was sent to Alister Hardy.

By the next morning the split had ended but opened up again (for the last time) that afternoon. 'The hedges still flickered with little live golden flames,' she recalled. The out-of-body-she stood on the cliffs looking across the sea to the setting sun as the other-she attended to the children. Then the two were merged again and 'the sunlight was a weak candle-glimmer to the light in which I must have been living without knowing it'.

CHAPTER FIVE

Nor Is It ...

Is the drugged brain the same as the mystic mind? Stace thought so after interviewing an American, described only as an 'intellectual', who'd had what he thought was a mystical experience after swallowing mescalin. He'd been standing at the window overlooking the garden (or yard) of a run-down tenement. 'The buildings were decrepit and ugly, the ground covered with boards, rags, and debris. Suddenly every object in my field of vision took on a curious and intense kind of existence of its own; that is, everything appeared to have an 'inside' – to exist as I existed, having inwardness, a kind of individual life, and every object, seen under this aspect, appeared exceedingly beautiful. There was a cat out there, with its head lifted, effortlessly watching a wasp that moved without moving just above its head. Everything was urgent with life . . which was the same in the cat, the wasp, the broken bottles, and merely manifested itself differently in these individuals (which did not therefore cease to be individuals however). All things seemed to glow with a light that came from within them.'

Laski has a whole chapter on drugs and the mystic vision. Few people in England took drugs in the '50s so all she had to go on were books and newspaper articles. Aldous Huxley's *The Doors of Perception* (about mescalin) came out in 1954, R H Ward's *A Drug-Taker's Notes* (about LSD) in '57. There were also articles in the *Manchester Guardian, New Yorker, Sunday Times* and *The Observer*.

Both Huxley and Ward were curious about the drugged mind and mysticism. Huxley, a rather desiccated cerebral introvert, gave us one of our best over-views of mysticism without ever knowing what it was like. Mescalin he hoped

34

would show him. He thought it did: the Beatific Vision, he called it (a gift previously granted only to Moses and St Paul, Laski added drily, and inaccurately). Did Laski agree?

She begins with duration. Ecstatic moments are just that: moments – seconds long most usually. Half an hour is a very long time, and also very, very rare. What she calls the 'afterglow' can last as long, or longer, but not the experience itself. The drugged state, on the other hand, can last for hours. Also, the ecstatic mood can change from 'dread to delight' but never 'delight to dread' as it can with drugs.

The ecstatic moment is timeless but the spaced out are aware of time, they just don't care about it. (Laski concedes that Huxley spoke of 'timeless bliss' but points out he was versed in the vocabulary of mysticism.)

Ecstatics almost always think they've been in touch with the beautiful and valuable. Beauty of one kind or another is, of course, perhaps the most common trigger. With drugs, however, it's often the other way round: normal triggers not only don't work, they can be funny. Music, for example, left Huxley cold while Cézanne's self-portrait made him laugh. All the drug-takers said the same: Icons, music, poetry rarely worked. Picasso didn't 'fit together', one man said, perhaps in an Emperor's clothes moment of honesty. (Has Picasso ever triggered a mystic moment in anyone?)

Non-triggers, Laski goes on (wrongly), are turned into triggers: Huxley's trousers, for example, and chair legs and curtains. She's on shaky ground here, I think: almost anything can be a trigger. And when it comes to walls she's way off beam. Huxley, for example, wrote about a 'blank but unforgettably beautiful' stucco'd wall, 'empty but charged with all the meaning and mystery of existence.' Ward, too, found 'astonishing beauty in a plain distempered wall'. To be fair, Laski in a footnote does draw attention to da Vinci's advice to painters to look for signs of divinity in damp walls. Walls in sunshine, or in shadow and shade, are enormously evocative of adamic level undertones.

Things 'glowed' for Huxley with bright colours which gave them a profound significance. He describes a deckchair 'with

35

stripes of deep but glowing indigo alternated with stripes of iridescence so intensely bright that they could not be made of anything but blue fire.' His words in themselves are a mild undertone-generator. Colour – just swatches of pure colour – can act as triggers or switches on their own.

Other differences? Ecstatics don't hallucinate or have bad trips. Ecstatics 'rejoice and feel delight at perfection': drugged people 'often burst out laughing at what is awry'. (Huxley laughed at a blue car till the tears ran down. 'Man had created that thing in his own image.') 'In ecstasy,' Laski ends, 'there is no fun whatsoever.' As if to compensate, most people after an ecstatic moment feel a universal love: Huxley, on the other hand, found people 'enormously irrelevant'. (Although to introverts people often are.) With mescalin there was no loss of ego: in fact ego, gets bigger until the drugged person becomes unfeeling, losing a sense of right and wrong.

Laski's was a paper exercise. Twenty years later the Transpersonal psychologist Stanislav Grof used real LSD on real people. He called the drug: 'an amplifier, or catalyst, of mental processes which facilitate the emergence of unconscious material from different levels of the human psyche'. By then a new word had also been coined – *entheogen* (from the Greek for 'god-created-within') – for any drug which induced 'non-ordinary states of consciousness'. Grof coined his own word – holotropic: 'moving towards wholeness'. This movement was caused by what he called 'holotropic breath work' – hyperventilating until the brain is nearly completely starved of oxygen and the body is close to death. But is the result a true mystic state or just the pathology of a dying brain? Mystic events occur when the mind – not the brain – is closed down.

Part Two

Crossing the Border?

Were they or weren't they? With some people it's hard to tell if they were, or are, mystics at all. Was Pugin? Edward Fitzgerald? James Thomson? Or William Morris who thought he wasn't but who maybe was?

CHAPTER SIX

Pugin – Martha or Secret Friend?

Ruskin and Pugin are both credited with starting the Gothic Revival – Ruskin theorised: Pugin built. Ruskin did so because he was a mystic who saw the spiritual in Gothic stone. But what of Pugin? Was he a Martha or a Secret Friend?

Ruskin (1819-1900) disliked Pugin: Pugin (1812-1852) shrugged. Augustus Welby Northmore Pugin was, in fact, an altogether more colourful man. By the age of twenty – still short of his majority – he'd been a ship wrecked smuggler, a furniture designer to the King, jailed for debt, and was a widower with a baby daughter. Even at the end of a hectic life he ran a part-time salvage operation from his cliff-top house above Ramsgate, as well as doing a bit of smuggling (of antiquities) on the side.

Ruskin, although once married, is thought to have died a virgin. Pugin, on the other hand, was so highly sexed he couldn't live without a woman. In his late teens, as a stage hand and scenery painter in London theatres, he must have slept with dozens: he was only seventeen when he married an eighteen year old actress (as she probably was). In the end, he had three wives and eight children. Most tellingly, when his second wife died he quickly courted the next great love of his life and then, when she turned him down, immediately began wooing the new great love of his life, the woman who did marry him.

Both Pugin and Ruskin died insane. The cause of Ruskin's madness seems unknown. Pugin's was probably syphilis, caught most likely in his theatre days – the timing was right: about twenty years from infection to the tertiary stage.

Ruskin was born rich. Pugin was born broke. Ruskin's father sold sherry. Pugin's drew pictures for a fashion magazine in pre-Revolutionary Paris: in exile in London he became an

38

architectural artist and a drawing master in a school for boys which he both set up and ran. Pugin's father hinted at – and his son outrightly claimed – descent from a Medieval Swiss nobleman, the Comte de Pugin. Pugin's English mother, on the other hand, really was quite well connected – Catherine Welby's family was prominent in Lincolnshire. (Would Ruskin Senior have had to go in by the Tradesman's Gate?)

Ruskin gave away his inherited money and then, without willing it, made another fortune from royalties on his books. Pugin died, if not broke then, strapped for cash, largely because his enormous lifetime earnings were spent as he went along. Next to his Ramsgate house, for example, he built a church with his own money.

Ruskin was an Oxford graduate. Pugin had no more than four years of inattentive schooling. On the other hand, he and his father sketched, and collected, bits of the ruins the French Revolution had made of Medieval Normandy. He grew into a rough kind of man, probably with a Cockney accent – he spelled 'various' with a 'w', just as Sam Weller pronounced it. He dressed, walked, talked and occasionally swore like a sailor.

Both Ruskin and Pugin were born Evangelicals. Ruskin dropped religion altogether, at least for a time. Pugin converted to Catholicism.

Both were artists. Pugin painted swiftly in watercolour – oil was too 'streaky' – taking between thirty minutes and an hour to complete a picture in the open air. On the other hand landscape didn't move him (it moved Ruskin to mystical ecstasies). Like Blake, Pugin illustrated his books with his own etchings.

Both wrote, though Ruskin was infinitely the better writer. Pugin's two most influential books were written in his twenties: *Contrasts* contrasts Medieval architecture with the squared off and shoddy buildings of his own day. He was still only twenty-nine when he wrote *The True Principles of Pointed or Christian Architecture* about the superiority of the Gothic. His books more than his buildings, he believed, 'revolutionised the taste of England'.

Ruskin was a thinker – the Welfare State grew out of his thought, to begin with. Although he had one or two world-changing ideas, it would strain the word to call Pugin that. All the same, he set in train practical ideas which shaped the following generations – a new Gothic style for schools and chapels, town halls and banks, a new kind of house for the richer middle classes, and thousands of patterns for everything from crockery to wall paper.

Ruskin played a small part in designing the Oxford Museum of Natural History (in Continental Gothic) but he could never match Pugin's genius for design and architecture: what could be more iconic than Big Ben's clock tower? His works, if not numberless, have never been properly numbered: they include cathedrals, churches (at least forty of them) with all their fonts, altars, rood screens, pulpits. He built stately homes, private houses, a parsonage, abbeys, a nunnery, almshouses and the internal decor of the House of Lords. On a smaller scale he designed iron work, wall paper, tiles, ceramics, stained glass, jewellery, fabrics, furnishings, chairs (including thrones), at least one banqueting hall, a chantry and a chimney piece.

Both Ruskin and Pugin argued against the pagan worthlessness of the Renaissance and for the fusion of life, work and spirit seen in medieval stone. Both argued for the spiritual superiority of the Gothic.

So was Pugin, like Ruskin, a mystic?

To Pugin, pagan architecture (the Square Style) symbolised death. It's a sham – stone should be itself, not imitation timber. The Renaissance was 'a huge mistake' which 'sapped the good out of everything' and which 'could live only so long as the Christian elements of truth lingered in it' because in the end it was 'destructive of all that is good in thought and material working.' 'This poisonous tree had to be uprooted before the Christian tree could flourish.' All of which Ruskin could have written, albeit with more subordinate clauses.

For Pugin, the spiritual was physically embodied in Gothic stone, and so reachable. Symmetry was wrong for the human mind. Gothic was natural because it's part of nature, something grown. In the Middle Ages, art, work, morals and religion fused into a completeness of life. What was right in society's soul was expressed, as a rightness, in stone. Great art and architecture come only from purity of the soul. In this Pugin could be paraphrasing Ruskin, in simpler sentences.

Pugin lived by one deep insight: everything has its own inner nature. To live properly you must abide by it, obey its rules. Gothic worked because it obeyed the rules governing the nature not only of stone but also of human life. These rules make for a wholeness of work, marriage, art, home, the spiritual. All this is readable in Gothic stone.

These unchanging, underlying rules Pugin called *True Principles* and he applied them to everything he worked on: churches, hospitals, houses, pottery, furnishings, furniture, glass, jewellery, wall paper. He even veto'd (bridegrooms could, apparently) the wedding dress of the one bride-to-be he never married. She'd chosen a pointed waist. 'It does not accord with the natural shape of the waist,' he told her. 'Nature is the true form.'

True Principles include charity, loyalty, community, care, hospitality, and also scholarliness and learning. By definition, using rules doesn't mean copying the past but applying them as if for the first time. The Grange, the house which he built for himself and his family on the sea cliffs above Ramsgate, doesn't look conventionally 'Gothic' but it is because it's based on True Principles, in this case the nature of human life and what makes for its wholeness. Not only is it supremely welcoming place, it's also satisfyingly grand without a trace of the slovenly or undisciplined: not so much a machine as a living thing for living in.

His son-in-law, Jonathan Powell, gives us two accounts of his own arrival at Pugin's house in Ramsgate one wild dark night just before Christmas, 1844. The first – possibly the true one because less Dickensianly dramatic – has him arriving, cold from an east wind, on the stage coach from Ashford (it was still pre-railway on the Isle of Thanet). In the other, a gale beat the Red Rover steam packet back from the North Foreland, forcing her into Margate harbour. Two cab drivers squabbled over the drenched, freezing and sea-sick boy (he was still only seventeen). The winner – all sea boots, oil skins, and whiskers – drove him off in an omnibus hauled by two jaded nags.

The door of The Grange had neither bell nor knocker. The boy kicked it. He heard the maids whispering together. Dare they open the door? 'Don't be such fools,' Pugin called to them. 'Do you want to be murdered?' The boy was too wet to care. 'Are you Powell?', Pugin shouted through the iron-barred spy-hole. When he answered 'yes', bolts, bars and locks were withdrawn, turned, unbolted, kicked.

Pugin, medium height but burly, stood there with a welcoming candle in his hand. Powell wore a *taglioni*, an overcoat fashionable at the time and named after a pair of ballet dancers. As he stood there, dripping, Pugin told him the *taglioni* would be 'blown to shreds on the pier' and tomorrow the boy must get clothes like his. He wore, habitually in the house, a sea-going suit of wool – jacket, 'roomy' trousers rolled up sailor-fashion, thick grey socks, heavy shoes, a neckerchief and a double breasted weskit. This was his office wear and seagoing rig, both.

Pugin's own day began at six when he unbolted the chapel door and knelt in front of the stone altar, carved with angels, for his own private prayers. Until seven thirty he worked in the library. In those first early days, the eldest boy Edward (Teddy he was nine when Powell arrived) stalked the house ringing a turn-out-of-bed bell. Day for the whole family, and servants, began with prayers in the chapel, the girls in veils, the boys in hoods. If there were no priest (at least two lived in from time to time), Pugin conducted the service, dressed in surplice and cassock, kneeling at a prie-dieu in front of the altar. Prayers like pop songs were short – three or four minutes – to hold the attention of the children: anything longer and they'd be pulling each other's hair, Pugin explained. 'Pater, Ave, Litany' were also short and quick for the same reason.

After prayers a crocodile of children carried their chairs from the dining room to the kitchen. Breakfast for them was bread and milk: for grown-ups (or older children like Powell) bread, butter and tea. Ham was eaten on Feast Days. Then Pugin went back to work, bending over his drawing board in the library with views of the flowerless garden and the sea. His was the shipshape orderly mind of a man whose workplace was cleared each evening, ready for the morning. When things went well he sang Gregorian chants and arias, imitating the opera stars of the day. (He was a good mimic: he told anecdotes with all the right voices.) On bad days, he'd talk to himself or shake his head out of the window. (He was on the road – or railway – a lot of the time, as well, overseeing his buildings.)

At eight in the evening the chapel bell was rung, calling the family to Compline. Supper was at nine – rice pudding, cheese, celery, water. Beer and tobacco, lit tobacco at least, were banned. Guests smoked outside. On a good day, leg of mutton was served. (A good day was defined as one with a big commission – a church, perhaps – in the morning mail.) Vegetables must have been dished up as well because, in a letter, Pugin rails against a villainous cook who'd boiled them hard as marble. Over supper Pugin read from *The Times*, chipping in with his own comments. At ten, doors were locked, barred and bolted, and the household went to bed.

As for his character, Powell gives two accounts. In the first, Pugin was open until deceived: in another he was suspicious of the whole species of lying humankind. For a time, he ran a school for Catholic children until he found they'd robbed him of thirty tons of coal. Yet once he took the shoes off his feet to give to an elderly beggar. He distinguished sharply between genuinely hurt and helpless people and idle scroungers – 'become a tailor,' he advised, 'rather than walk about asking for other's bread.'

He was always childlike, enthusiastic, humorous, downcast by disappointment, absorbed in ideas, unconventional. How else is he described? Frank, fearless and somebody to be wary of – a sharp brain, you sense, lurked behind that broad forehead which, given the firmness of the face, mouth and jaw, could cut probably you down with a word. Yet at the same time he was insecure and suspicious, a man who had to bolt the doors by ten o'clock to shut out a world of burglars, blackguards, murderers. He was full of fear – of loss, the dark, the unknown, ghosts. Late one evening he was seen in a corridor in the Catholic College in Oscott with two candles. Why not one? 'Suppose one blew out?'

Pugin had known Ramsgate from boyhood when he stayed there with his Aunt Selina, a lady of private means, on Rose Hill.

But something else drew him there (apart from the sea, without which he couldn't live): St Augustine, who brought Christianity back to England, made his landfall at Ebbsfleet, a mile or so down the coast, in 597. (The Isle of Thanet in those far-off days really had been an island, separated from the mainland by the Wantsum Channel, navigable all the way to the Thames by sea-going ships.) St Augustine founded both Canterbury Cathedral on the site of a Roman church, and also the great abbey outside the city walls. Minster then *was* a minster on the shore of the Wantsum sea. (It was a nunnery, abandoned when the Danes raided it once too often.)

Pugin planned to recreate something of St Augustine's spirit and achievement. The nucleus was to be a house, a church, and an abbey. As it turned out, the abbey was eventually built by his son Edward, the same Teddy whose bell rang sleepers out of bed all those years before. But Pugin himself built the church, out of best Whitby stone and Kentish flint, with his own money. He gave it to the Diocese of Southwark as a gift.

Finally, there's Pugin's lifelong passion for the sea. He bought his first boat – *Elizabeth* – when he was nineteen. His first voyage, with help, was down the Thames, a tricky river with great sweeping bends, packed at the time with ships under sail, and with a ferocious ebb tide. For most of the rest of his life he was a sea-going boatman. Also a smuggler. As a young man he brought over antiquities from France and Holland. To avoid paying tax, he avoided harbours. Once he was wrecked in the Firth of Forth.

In his last four years, he and a friend – Alfred Luck, widower, Catholic convert, tenant of his house after Pugin's death, and in the end a priest – co-owned a lugger, *Caroline*. She was a working boat – fishing, trips round the bay, salvage work in winter. Every now and then throughout the day Pugin would climb the tower of his house with a spy-glass to scan the Channel for ships in distress. A trap door in the hall opened not only into the cellar but also into a tunnel bored down through the chalk to the beach. (Whether Pugin dug it doesn't seem to be known. It's said he also used it to evade tax on antiquities he smuggled in from Europe.) All he had to do was run down the tunnel to

44

launch the lugger, though where the crew hung out has not been explained. *Caroline's* cost, seventy pounds, was repaid in one go after they salvaged the cargo of a Dutch galliot outward bound for Spain.

Pugin moved into The Grange with his six children on the death of his second wife, Louisa, in 1844. He married Jane Knill four years later. In the last days of his madness, Jane stayed, in disguise so as not to upset him, in the house in London where he was being treated for insanity with chloroform. 'Are you my wife?' he asked her one day. 'Thank you for taking care of me.' So she took him back to die in his own house by the sea.

It had been a crowded life revolving around religion (with a bit of crime on the side). So was Pugin a mystic? Against it are the opinions of his son-in-law – Pugin was *not* a spiritual man, he tells us: he was too practical. Also he 'accepted the mysteries of his Faith like a man of the Middle Ages, and with the same childlike awe of the Supernatural.' More strongly, he says Pugin 'never pretended to any spiritual inspiration, or opposed Ecclesiastical Authority.' His was 'a practical mind not given to pondering on what was beautiful in abstract.'

For the 'for' side, Powell speaks only obliquely. Pugin 'had an instinct for the beautiful in form and colour, and so we find poetic feeling in all his work'. And beauty, Ruskin believed, is part of the higher, imparting something of the spiritual.

Furthermore, Pugin could put 'into material form something of himself higher than knowledge or skill.' Even more interestingly he tells us how Pugin worked: very rapidly, his hand skimming over the paper ceaselessly, using only a two foot rule and a pencil. (One day a commission for stained glass for an Oxford college came in the first post: the finished design was mailed back at eleven o'clock the same morning.) 'It seemed as if his fingers were attached to his thoughts,' Powell says, strikingly. Japan was still a closed society in the 1840s, but this could be pure Zen: Pugin's fingers were attached not to thought but to No-Mind, the Buddha-Nature, Consciousness, or the well of all creativity. Which may just mean, of course, that he had a very large well of creativity to begin with.

More revealingly Powell writes: 'The internal and external

worlds, nature and human nature, interacted as powerfully as ever on him. Winter sunlight slanting through stained glass, as it might be in one of his father's watercolours, never failed to touch him. 'I have been frantic all day,' Pugin wrote in a letter to a friend, 'but a Ray of the sun setting on the chancel arch has restored tranquillity to my soul. Ever thine, vade in pace.''

And what we are to make of his vision of the Gothic as physically embodying the spiritual in soaring stone? It matches Ruskin's experience perfectly.

On balance, however, Pugin seems not to have been mystical. Which raises an interesting point: people who are mystically inclined often puzzle the non-mystical – but that works the other way around as well: the non-mystical puzzle the mystical. To them, theistic religion is barely tenable without a spiritual underpinning – so what did a non-mystical Martha like Pugin get out of pointed architecture and applied art?

CHAPTER SEVEN

'An Old Man in a Dry Month'

B ut can people be mystical without knowing it? Was Edward Fitzgerald? He's the man who gave us the profoundly unspiritual translation of *The Rubaiyat of Omar Khayyam* whose 'eat, drink and be merry' philosophy appealed so enormously to a secular world. Although little read today, it remains the best selling translated poem in the language, perhaps the most sold poem in English ever. Omar Khayyam Clubs were set up all over England and America. Conan Doyle, Edmund Gosse and Arthur Pinero belonged to the same one in London. They were pretty lively places, too, by all accounts, probably because the stanzas can be declaimed:

> Come, fill the Cup, and in the Fire of Spring
> The Winter Garment of Repentance fling:
> The Bird of Time has but a little way
> To fly – and Lo! the Bird is on the Wing.
>
> The moving finger writes; and, having writ,
> Moves on: nor all thy piety nor wit
> Shall lure it back to cancel half a line,
> Nor all thy tears wash out a word of it.

Chesterton thought the poem was evil. Browning wrote *Rabbi Ben Ezra* in reply to it. As late as the 1950s young men got it off by heart. It is 'Savage against Destiny', FitzGerald said of it, 'Epicurean in its Pathos.' It expresses, he thought, what everybody feels at the bottom of their hearts. Benson (Fitzgerald's biographer) thought it the most beautiful expression of both agnosticism and the Epicureanism which comes with it.

But it isn't agnostic or Epicurean at all. Omar Khayyam was

a follower of Sufism, Islam's mystic wing, and his *rubaiyat* (it means 'quatrains') are mystical. The wine-drunkenness is spiritual intoxication, the mystic moment which leads to knowledge of the Divine. All the same, although he missed the esoteric meaning of this poem, Fitzgerald may well been a bit of an adamic mystic himself.

He was was born Edward Purcell, in 1809, in Suffolk. His parents were first cousins. Both were Anglo-Irish. John Purcell was a descendant of Oliver Cromwell and his wife's ancestry included the Earls of Kildare. In 1818, when she became the richer of the two through an inheritance, Purcell adopted her maiden name for the whole family. (Edward never liked it.) Between them they owned estates in Lancashire, Suffolk, Sussex, Northamptonshire, and Ireland. They had eight children. Edward was seventh.

His childhood was happy, he claimed, full of incident and adventure. The boy knew Paris, loved the sea, the theatre, books, and the countryside, huge tracts of which his family owned. He was a lifelong collector of friends. He made them early and late throughout his life. 'I am an idle fellow,' he said of himself many years later, 'of a very ladylike turn of sentiment: and my friendships are more like loves, I think.' (Asked, when he was nearing his own end, who had been the friend he loved most, Tennyson replied: 'Why, old Fitz, to be sure.')

At Cambridge Fitz settled into his lifelong dilettante ways: pottering, dabbling, picking up and putting down the classics, painting watercolours, playing the organ, reading and writing poetry, without any system or aim. Already, too, he was unkempt, dishevelled and badly dressed. When his mother called (in a coach and four) he had no boots to put on to meet her. He was, of course, well off (Carlyle claimed he gave Tennyson at least three hundred pounds a year at this time). After going down, without a degree, he began a drifting life: parties, visits, travel, breakfasts, the theatre.

Then, in 1837, he moved permanently to Suffolk where his father had recently bought Boulge Park by the River Deben. FitzGerald took over a two-roomed lodge in the grounds. He had a bust of Shakespeare, a dog, a cat, Beauty Bob (a parrot), and two servants: an old soldier who'd served at Waterloo and his snuff-taking wife. All that and a barrel of beer. The place was a shambles and he was unshaven and slovenly. 'What will become of him in this world?' a friend from his Grammar School days asked.

A new friendship in 1846 with Edward Cowell, the twenty year old son of an Ipswich corn merchant, led him to *Omar Khayyam*. Young Cowell, who was spoke Spanish, Sanskrit and Farsi, was married to an older woman of private means. FitzGerald visited them in Ipswich where they would sit in the garden (with its monkey puzzle tree and path leading to a mill) reading Spanish, Persian, and Greek. Mrs Cowell wrote poetry: FitzGerald criticised it. Then, when he and his wife moved to Oxford, Cowell came across a manuscript of Omar Khayyam's verses in the Bodleian. It was written in purple-black ink on yellow paper powdered all over with gold. He gave a transcript to FitzGerald who, typically, put if aside for ten years before translating it, and only then with Cowell's help: Fitz's Farsi, like his Spanish, was never very good. The Cowells were in India part of the time: help was asked for and given by letters sent back and forth in P&O mail steamers.

In 1860, now fifty-one, Fitzgerald moved into rooms above the gun-maker's shop in Woodbridge market and bought a seagoing yacht called *The Scandal* (because it was the staple of conversation in the town), marvelling at how his skipper never stopped smiling though the father of twins. He took to the water, he said, because the country all around was the graveyard of his friends, and the new generation of landowners was destroying the landscape to make money. Sailing to Aldburgh was a favourite trip. He still delighted in the speech of country people: a sailor said of his boat that she 'go like a violin' and 'all is calm as a clock' after a gale had dropped.

In 1864 he bought a farmhouse near Woodbridge, and then, typically, left it empty for ten years, apart from workmen who added rooms and walls and then knocked them down again as his whims came and went. Six acres of fields were turned into woods. That year too he made a friend of a Lowestoft fisherman called 'Posh' Fletcher. 'This is altogether the Greatest Man I have known,' he enthused, idealising Posh as a leader of men of the finest Saxon stock. 'A man,' he added, 'of simplicity of soul, justice of thought, tenderness of nature, a gentleman of Nature's grandest type.' ('It must be confessed,' said Benson, 'that a good deal of sentimentality was wasted over this sea-lion.') Fitz built Posh a herring lugger, *The Meum and Tuum*.

In the 1870s he moved into his farmhouse, propelled by eviction from his lodgings. His landlord, Mr Berry, had become engaged to a widow. 'Old Berry would now have to be called Old Gooseberry,' Fitzgerald observed. The widow got to hear of it: he had to go. On eviction day she stood at the foot of the stairs calling up: 'Be firm, Berry! Remind him of what he called you.'

In the farmhouse, he lived in the downstairs parlour. The organ, which he played from memory without sheet music, was in the hall. The living room was his library. The rest of the house, with added rooms, was furnished and open at all times to his nieces, though they rarely met.

When his sight began to fail, he hired a local boy to read to him of an evening. Benson writes: 'Here he sits, in a dry month, old and blind, being read to by a country boy, longing for rain.' (T S Eliot turned the lines into: 'Here I am, an old man in a dry month/Being read to by a boy, waiting for rain.' Both passages are full of undertones: Benson, though, has the edge.) While being read to, Fitz would sit by the fire place in a dressing gown, slippered feet on the fender, wearing a top hat (from which he occasionally took a red silk handkerchief), snuff box in his hand, stroking his beard with a paper-knife.

He was almost teetotal, almost a vegetarian (out of courtesy he ate meat in other people's houses). At home he lived on apples, pears, bread, sometimes a turnip, cheese, and milk pudding. Tea was his favourite meal, at least in company, with country butter and bread. He smoked a clay pipe – presumably a long churchwarden – which he broke into pieces after a single use. He loved colours – bright curtains and carpets, butterflies, moths and birds (he kept a multi-coloured mop for years as a kind of sculpture). He loved birdsong (except the nightingale which, he said, should be in bed like everybody else). He also loved 'church bells, the wind in the trees, rattle of ropes, the sharp hiss of the sea.'

He was a tall unkempt man in baggy sailor-blue clothes. In hot weather he carried his shoes on a stick over his shoulder. One woman observed he was proud, but not too proud to carry his boots to the cobblers to be mended. He was not popular with local people who called him 'soft in the head' and 'dotty'. He could also be peevish, pettish, grumpy, intolerant of having his comfort or habits disturbed, tetchy, and even bad-tempered. Once he asked the local bookseller to dinner. When the man arrived, FitzGerald turned him from the door. 'I saw you yesterday,' he wrote in a letter of apology the next morning, 'but I was not fit for company, and felt that I could not be bothered.'

FitzGerald was a man for small things: vignettes and glimpses, impressions. Big things like the work of Milton, Browning or Thackeray were too much for him. In music he preferred Handel – simple but grand. He had a strong sense of *lachrymae rerum* – tears for things, the sadness of things, 'the endless pathos of the world.' His delight in small things and their pathos – the glance of sunlight on a leaf, caught and then gone – was spoiled by knowing it couldn't last. He was unwilling to suffer, Benson believed, and so couldn't write great poetry except once, in *The Rubaiyat* when he faced up to the darkness below life. He read, Benson said, to deaden pain.

Benson also claimed he had the insight for lyrical poetry but not the words. If he didn't write mystical nature poetry, the makings of it are certainly in his letters. One June, in a letter to Cowell, he described the greenness outside his bedroom window, the scent of hay, the sound of whetstone on scythe, and the roses already passing away. His feeling for things was deep. Here are three quotations from letters to friends, the first in 1842:

> 'I get radishes to eat for breakfast of a morning: with them comes a savour of earth that brings all the delicious gardens of the world back into one's soul, and almost draws tears from my eyes.'

> 'The trees murmur a continuous soft chorus to the solo which my soul discourses in.'

> 'There's no sea like the Aldburgh Sea. It talks to me.'

All these things could indicate an undertone-level, an adamic level, mystic. His life story, too, is rich in undertones.

CHAPTER EIGHT

News from Somewhere

Laski, for one, had no doubts at all that some people can be mystics without knowing it. William Morris was, she thought. Yet whoever heard of a socialist mystic? The mystic has a lone vision of the spiritual, the socialist of a collectivised materialism. William Morris called himself a socialist although his novel, *News from Nowhere*, is far from the reality of socialist rule. It's the story of a London (and an England beyond it) returned to a simplicity and honesty no human society ever has, or ever could, sustain. There are no politics, no schools, no money – only peace, love and purity in a very loose, un-Statist utopia. (The Houses of Parliament are barns for storing manure, handy for boats on the river.)

But *News from Nowhere,* Laski maintained, isn't really political at all: it's an adamic vision of Edenic innocence in a society were the crooked timber of mankind has been chain-sawed out and carted away. If she's right, it would mean that Morris's socialism was spiritual rather than political. Personal anguish for a lost Arcadia drove him on as much, if not more, than pity for the down-trodden or hatred of his middle class peers. Certainly it would mean he wasn't irreligious at all (he was an atheist) but was esoterically spiritual, without knowing it. It could be. He was a disciple of John Ruskin who, in his first incarnation as mystic and champion of all things Gothic and Medieval, believed that beauty itself is spiritual. So Morris's plan to make beautiful items through his Arts and Crafts Movement may also have been spiritually inspired, though I doubt he'd have thanked you for telling him so.

52

This state of mind, Laski goes on, is probably at the bottom of all utopia-mongering and therefore also of H G Wells's *In the*

Days of the Comet. In that novel, people who survive the disaster are changed, ready to create a perfect new world. These new feelings, Wells says, are like 'glowing moments' brought on 'by histories and music and beautiful things, by heroic instances and splendid stories'.

Laski also claimed George Gissing for mysticism – not an obvious choice: he was a novelist of poverty and squalor, commercialism and exploitation. Far from being a socialist, he believed in an 'aristocracy of brains'. In 1875, still a student in Owens College (now Manchester University), he was jailed for stealing money to give to a prostitute he'd befriended and later married. He wrote poorly paid novels, one a year at one time, and short stories to scrape a bare living. His second wife became insane and was shut away. Only in his last few years (he died in 1903 aged forty-six) did he find any happiness – with a French woman he bigamously married and with whom he lived in the French Basque country. He's buried in St Jean de Luz – St John of Light. Yet even Gissing, Laski believed, had at least one ecstatic episode which he described in a novel. To get away from the bad air, food and misery of London, Gissing makes one of his characters impulsively catch a train to Devon. There he has a classic ecstatic experience – 'loss of the feelings of self, of worldliness, of time, gain of feelings of new life, joy, knowledge', as Laski puts it.

Elsewhere in the her book, she distinguishes between euphoria and the genuine thing. They can very easily be confused. Edward Gibbon, author of *The Decline and Fall of the Roman Empire*, was an Age of Reason atheist. Unknown to himself, Laski argued, he might also have been a lesser kind of mystic. She quotes a passage from his *Autobiography*:

'My temper is not very susceptible of enthusiasm, and the enthusiasm which I do not feel I have ever scorned to affect. But, at the distance of twenty-five years, I can neither forget nor express the strong emotions which agitated my mind as I first approached and entered the eternal city. After a sleepless night, I trod, with a lofty step, the ruins of the Forum; each memorable spot where Romulus stood, or Tully spoke, or Caesar fell, was at once present to my eye; and several days of intoxication were lost or enjoyed before I could a cool and minute investigation.'

Was this mysticism? The passage, I must say, reads more like prolonged excitement. On the other hand, there's no reason why excitement can't be a trigger in its own right. If it's deep enough, it could stop thought and get rid of the ego.

I should add that, conversely, the exoterically minded can also mistake mysticism for something more worldly. People of a statist cast of mind, for example, often mistake the mystic's otherworldliness for a wish for state ownership. Certainly socialists often quote the 17th century Levellers and Diggers as their political forebears, believing they all shared a craving for the abolition of private property. But Gerard Winstanley, the Digger leader, was a mystic. Once you've had a deep enough mystic experience, you're free of the need for ownership. But mysticism is a minority pursuit and the problem of other people remains: most would still want to own things. On top of that, there's mammalian nature – what do you do with the Alpha Male? All pack mammals, including humans, have them. There can be no equality as long as they're around (and no society at all if they vanish).

CHAPTER NINE

Mystic Manqué?

Some of the unlikeliest people can recognise, and applaud, mysticism in others. Does that mean there's a streak of it in them too? James Thomson (BV) is mainly known now for *The City of Dreadful Night,* perhaps the most desolate poem about spiritual emptiness every written in English. His own life he called 'a long defeat' and 'poison mixed with gall'.

> The world rolls round for ever like a mill;
> It grinds out death and life and good or ill;
> It has no purpose, heart or mind or will.

But:

> This little life is all we must endure,
> The grave's most holy place is ever sure,
> We fall asleep and never wake again.

He made a living of sorts as a journalist writing mainly for two magazines – *The National Reformer* and *Cope's Tobacco Plant* – but too often he was bitter and childish in his attacks on religion: God, he once wrote, is 'a desperately sharp shaver and a terrible fellow for going to law'. Yet in 1866 he wrote – in *The National Examiner* – a wonderfully insightful review of Gilchrist's *Life of Blake.*

'Blake was always poor in the world's wealth, always rich in spiritual wealth, happy and contented and assured, living with God.' 'He was a thoroughly healthy and happy religious soul, whose happiness was thoroughly unselfish and noble.' Most religious believers, Thomson goes on, try to 'argue themselves and others into a sort of belief in a sort (and such a sort!) of deity'. But Blake *saw* God clearly and unmistakably and so disdained 'the pretensions of gropers and guessers who are blind'.

55

In one sentence, Thomson anticipates the ideas of both William James and Bergson. People, he writes, will say Blake's belief was an illusion. 'But an illusion constant and self-consistent and harmonious with the world throughout the whole of a man's life, wherein does this differ from a reality?' 'Blake and Swedenborg and other true mystics (Jesus among them) undoubtedly had senses other than ours. It is futile for us to argue against the reality of their perception as it would be false in us to pretend that our perceptions are the same.'

Sects clash only because they're all on the same low plane but Blake was as unlike 'common Christians' as he was unlike 'common atheists'. Perceptively as well, Thomson noticed that Blake's object (in *Auguries of Innocence*) 'was not to expand a small fact into a universal truth, but to concentrate the full essence of a universal truth into a small fact.'

Of the *Prophetic Books,* Thomson argues that anybody who lives an isolated and introverted life 'comes to give a quite peculiar significance to certain words and phrases and emblems'. Metaphors and symbols which to the common run of writers are merely 'handy counters' were for Blake 'burdened with rich and various freights of spiritual experience.' To Blake, these words and symbols were like a ship which he needed to carry him across an unknown sea to an unknown shore. People reading him for the first time see only the storm-battered hull – they find the words and symbols 'obscure and ludicrous'.Unknown to Thomson (most probably), the boat is also a Zen metaphor – a ferry to take you to a meeting with the mystic moment on the far shore, there to be beached and abandoned, no longer needed. Thomson ends with a few thoughts about Blake's more difficult poetry. If you find 'sincerity and wisdom and beauty' in his easy early work, you should persevere with the harder later poems.

I've told Thomson's story briefly in *Undertones: Mild Mysticism in an Age of Umber.* His life was a disaster from beginning to end. Edwin Adams, a journalist and a friend of Bradlaugh's, summed him up as 'a man of gloomy aspect, manners, and ideas. Even his smile was sad. It seemed as if he was suffering from an irrepressible sorrow. Life to him was not a mission, but a mistake.' Yet BV, as we've just seen, also saw with clarity the mysticism in Blake. Does this mean that, given a better break in life, he might have had mystical leanings or even mystical moments? In other words, was he a mystic manqué? Incompleteness might explain the sheer depth of his despair.

CHAPTER TEN

Silence, Stillness, Light

S adness and repose are at the centre of all mystical art. They're always there, without exception. Few things illustrate this fact more clearly than the paintings of the Danish artist Vilhelm Hammershøi. His art is undoubtedly mystical, at the adamic level: but was he?

Stillness is in everything he did from first to last. His was the genius of the emptiness which is fullness. Silence and stillness seem to have been wired into the man himself, not just his art. Rilke (who was a mystic) visited him in Copenhagen in 1904 to gather material for an essay. Hammershøi hardly spoke. In an interview in 1907 (one of only two he ever gave) he did say he was interested in lines. Lines and light, but mainly lines. He always began with lines until he had a framework to be filled with oils. Colour interested him less. Even his landscapes and outdoor scenes are drained of it. His portraits are of darkly dressed and pale faced people. White and grey are his main colours, shifting along the spectrum in minute steps. Grisaille is the painter's word for it – a near monochrome, usually of grey or brown. With these colours he painted the mystery at the heart of things.

Hammershøi was either a shop-keeper's or a wholesaler's or a merchant's son (accounts vary) who was born in Copenhagen in 1864. From the age of eight he had private drawing lessons and at fifteen enrolled in the Royal Danish Academy of Fine Art. In addition, he also studied at a break-away school, De Frie Studieskoler (*frie* in the sense of independent, not fee-free) which had been set up by disgruntled students in 1882. His teacher, P S Krøyer, was one of the Skagen school of painters. In an early portrait Hammershøi gives Krøyer a fierce beetle-browed bearded face, a bit like D H Lawrence minus the blood and sex philosophy. Krøyer's own later self-portrait shows a benign man with a pointed ginger beard and pince-nez painting at an easel against a backdrop of kindly blue sea and sky. Who was the more accurate?

In 1891, aged twenty-seven, Hammershøi married Ida Ilsted and for the next twenty-odd years painted her endlessly – sometimes from the front, mostly from the back, as she stood or sat in stillness in almost empty rooms. They lived semireclusively all their married lives in flats in the old port area of Copenhagen. He died in 1916 of cancer.

His work can be split into two: those pieces which are mildly mystic-inducing, and those which aren't. On the whole the outdoor paintings don't work, not mystically at least. His pale or lead coloured landscapes don't work in that way at all: flat fieldless spits of land, flat lead-grey strips of sea, flat lead-grey landfalls beyond.

The exception is the painting of Christianborg Palace in the winter of early 1900 or late 1899. There's a canal or canalised grey, unflowing river of off-white ice, with off-white snow lying on straight grey buildings. The lines of windows are grey and dead-eyed. The bridge across the dead river leads to a gate flanked by snow-covered, bell-like domes. Unsmoking chimneys are like Wren spires in the City and in the painting serve the same silent purpose, pointing upwards to the unknown. These are chimneys with no fires in the grates below and so serving no purpose in a cold climate in wintertime. There are no footprints in the snow on the path above the river, and an unused door is shut tight. This is high latitude painting, all low light and snow.

Ten years earlier, in 1890/1, he'd painted the same palace, snow-free, in late Autumn. The roofs are no longer off-white but blue and red. The blue one is a mansard above yellow walls. The domes over the gate posts are spiky with statues which are not obvious in the snow scene. The river or canal is tinged with green. It's the same palace, yet not the same – its other-worldliness has gone and taken that desolation mysticism with it.

Stillness, as I've already said, was Hammershøi's stock in

59

trade. He could even paint stillness in faces, though presumably the stillness was in him, not his sitters. A cellist is so still you can't imagine his bow ever scraping across the strings: this painting is not about sound, but silence. More disquieting is the 1907 portrait of Ida stirring a cup of coffee with a spoon while staring into an unknown distance. She wears a v-necked dress and has a prominent nose and eyes and straggling hair. She's not good looking, and in fact leaves an impression of a Van Gogh painting in his potato-eating phase. There is a peasant look about her. Her left, clenched, hand is laid tiredly on the table by the white cup. Is it the stillness of defeat? Is it right, you feel, to be looking at her at all?

Most of their lives were passed in the old port area of Copenhagen with its wharves for blue water ships and global trade. Strand Street must have been busy (there was a marine engineering workshop at one end) but it meant nothing to him as a painter: his genius was an indoors one. They had two flats linked by a bridge across an alley. The flats were a maze of rooms which appear in over sixty paintings, some with Ida, some without. Most show only her back and her long black frock and slender neck with dark hair combed up above the nape. Props and venues are repeated. Here's Ida playing an upright piano (or spinnet?) sitting in a white spoke-backed chair with a white clothed table in front with two white plates and yellow butter on a white dish. Another painting has Ida standing next to the piano with her knee on a chair looking through a window through which light pours.

Hammershøi began this theme of stillness, Ida and light early in his career. The year before they married he painted a bedroom scene which scandalised the Academicians. It shows the back of Ida as she stands looking through a window in a bedroom with twin beds with white coverlets. One of the beds is brass. The focus is on Ida in black, narrow waisted, narrow hipped, hair up, more of a wraith than a woman. The window is made triangular by white curtains and she gazes into a vagueness of outdoor light and bare sketchy trees. Hammershøi went on re-painting this basic scene of a darkly clad woman's back, whiteness and greyness, perspective and light for the next twenty years. These paintings are unparalleled, his 'monuments to unageing intellect.'

At least five paintings feature the same corner of a room with the same door and window. It's a white room with sunlight shining through the small panes of a sash window (though no catch is shown). In 1900 Ida, in black, sits reading with her back to the easel as sunlight shines unheeded through the curtained window. Light in the shape of the window lies on the floor, half a pane cut out by the shadow of the curtain. The white door is bright with reflected light from the floor. Above her head, a painting hangs on the wall: a grey square in a white square in a brown frame. Six years later the painter's eye has panned slightly to the right in the same, now curtainless, room. It's bare but not empty, filled as it is with direct and reflected light. Light re-makes the window panes silently on the floor. Sunlight is reflected on the white painted door. Three years later, in 1909, the same room reappears. Now we see Ida's back as she sits at a desk looking through the window. Dust motes lie in complete stillness in the sun beam which is broken in straight lines by the bars of the window. Another painting shows the same room along with Ida, unusually facing the painter, looking down at her sewing. A polished table stands between her and the easel. To her left, the window is over-spilling with light. Switch back to 1900 and here is the same room in the evening. Strong sunlight slants in from the left. The room is again empty save for sunlight and paint and light reflected from it. A ripple of roof tiles and a window can be made out through the bright panes of glass and sunlight. The door must open on to the room which was also a bridge joining the two sides of the flat across the intervening alleyway.

Perhaps the most mind-stilling paintings are of vistas in all their variety – through open doors or empty rooms to a distant line or blaze of light: looking through emptiness to an eternity of light: vistas, views, through a maze of rooms and open doors always leading through stillness into light. In some, Ida stands with her back to the spectator. As a finger pointing to the light? Or a painted spectator like you, the living one outside the frame? Are both of you looking through emptiness into light? Where

John Donne found that love for a woman 'makes one little roome, an every where', a Hammershøi roome leads you beyond space and time. Was he an introvert whose inner world was more real than the outer? Was he a mystic or just the cause of mysticism in others?

Part Three

William Blake (1757-1827)

Blake was a throw-back. The 19th century West was strangely rich in artistic mystics but Blake was a complete standalone: nobody else was at all like him – the others were children of the Enlightenment, Blake was a child of Late Antiquity and the Middle Ages. He'd never really been to school but was well-read in Hermeticism, Alchemy, Paracelsus, Jacob Boehme and Swedenborg. He taught himself to read some Greek, Latin, French and Italian but he came across Neoplatonism in Thomas Taylor's translations of Plotinus and Proclus. (Blake and Taylor were almost exactly the same age. For a time they were friends.)

He was a Cockney who lived almost all his life in two or three streets on the edge of Soho and by The Strand. His father sold stockings for a living in Broad (now Broadwick) Street and Blake was born above the shop. Blake's wife was the illiterate daughter of a market gardener in Battersea (which show just how small London was in the late 18th century). The greatest loss in his life seems to have been the death at nineteen of his brother Robert when Blake was in his thirties. He watched his brother's ghost rising through the ceiling, clapping. (It isn't always easy to take Blake seriously. Was he ever really quite right in the head?) Still, life as ever moved on although with Blake that was never very far – in this case to a house in Poland Street, a hundred yards away.

Blake was also a late starter: he began his life's work in his early thirties, around 1788 or so. Within eight years the bulk of it was done. He began small: his first etchings – *There Is No Natural Religion* and *All Religions Are One* – are tiny (perhaps dictated by the price of copper) and they set out a simple mysticism and philosophy. Next year, 1789, he etched his first Illuminated

Books: *Songs of Innocence* and *The Book of Thel*. At thirty-four he began *The Marriage of Heaven and Hell*.

Then he and his wife moved into a large cottage with a big garden in Lambeth, south of the river. (The story of the Blakes being caught under a vine arbour stark naked save for helmets (on their heads) seems to be untrue). There, over the next seven years, he etched the emblems now called *The Gates of Paradise*. He also finished *The Marriage of Heaven and Hell*, and began and finished *Visions of the Daughters of Albion*: *America, A Prophecy*: *Songs of Innocence and of Experience*: *The First Book of Urizen*: *Europe, A Prophecy*: *The Song of Los*: *The Book of Ahania*: *The Book of Los* and *Vala or The Four Zoas*. He also, in 1796/7, designed and engraved the illustrations for Young's *Night Thoughts*: they were never published and aren't very good. His engravings for Gray's collected poems are. Gray was an Augustan eliding into a Romantic, a man more after Blake's own heart.

Only once did Blake live outside London. When he was forty-two, John Flaxman, the sculptor, introduced him to William Hayley, a squire with poetic pretensions and property on the Sussex coast. The following the year Hayley, gave Blake a job along with a tied cottage in Felpham near Bognor Regis by the sea. London then was geographically still rather small: the fields of Kent and Surrey were close but this was Blake's first and, apart from short stays late in life in Kent, almost only taste of rural landscape. He saw its mystic possibilities, though he never followed up on them: he was a Cockney through and through.

In Felpham he illustrated Hayley's books of verse but things weren't going too well when he ran into Trooper Schofield of the Royal Dragoons who, it seems, had been asked by Hayley's gardener to mow Blake's lawn. Blake, who hated kings and English soldiers (those of other nationalities he seems to have approved of), threw him out and he was charged with sedition because of what Schofield said he'd said while doing so – i.e. 'Damn the King, and damn his soldiers, they are all slaves'. The jury at Chichester Assizes acquitted him.

Another friend, Thomas Butts, supported him for years by buying every painting or etching he cared to make. Ironically, given Blake's pacifist hatred of soldiers, Butts was chief clerk in the Muster Master's office, a busy man presumably in a time of world war with huge troop movements criss-crossing the globe. Butts however may have made money from property and the stock market and was rich enough to pay Blake a guinea a time for pictures – nearly three hundred in the end: whole walls in his Fitzroy Square house must have been covered with them. Butts was no artist and no mystic yet he saw something in Blake which more exalted men failed to see.

Blake, in fact, needed all the help he could get: he was a man who was easily cheated and so was rooked more often than not. From Felpham, the Blakes moved back to London, to rooms – no house, no cottage – in South Molton Street (in the triangle between New Bond and Oxford Streets). Once there, he was commissioned to illustrated Blair's *The Grave*. He drew the designs but the engraving was given to Luigi Schiavonetti, (quite a few Italians lived in London at the time). Schiavonetti made £500, the publisher Cromeck £1,800. Blake got £20.

In 1809 Blake was fifty-two and fairly well known to other artists though not the buying public. Perhaps in desperation he held his one and only one-man exhibition in rooms above the hosiery shop in Broad Street where he'd been born. It flopped.

Income then seems to have dried up almost altogether. Certainly, when he was in his early sixties, Blake and his wife moved to even cheaper rooms in Fountains Court – no longer in existence but it was off The Strand down by the river. He made the woodcuts to illustrate Thornton's edition of Virgil's *Eclogues* (which inspired *The Ancients,* that brotherhood of mystic painters who lived in Shoreham in Kent). The publishers, being coarse men, rejected his work and gave the blocks to their regular workmen to re-cut. They were saved when Thornton himself stepped in and told them to honour their contract with the old man.

At seventy, the year he died, Blake was learning Italian to help him illustrate Dante. Dante's Hell, of course, he saw as being here on an earth twisted out of shape by Reason, Rules and Ego. A few days before he died, he coloured in a print of his *Ancient of Days*. His last drawing – of his wife, Kate – is lost. He was buried in Bunhill Fields, where Bunyan also lay.

CHAPTER ELEVEN

Et in Ulro, Ego

Understanding the basic Blake is easy – at bottom he's a standard mystic. Ego and the thinking mind, he knew (as all mystics do), stops us from seeing divinity. Strip out the Ego, therefore, and stop thinking and you'll see it (it's almost mechanical). According to Blake this is because each of us is God. For him this wasn't a metaphor either, but the literal truth. We *are* God. (Blake was a Christian of sorts – the sort the Inquisition burned: for him Christianity was all about forgiveness.) Each of us is therefore immortal. We know death only because we're born into it: this world *is* death – in fact, it's the only death we'll ever know. But even in this death-life we can get back to Wholeness and Paradise. Art is the way. Art is itself a divine revelation.

He also *almost* wrote a great epic for the modern West. What would the world be like if, for two hundred years, we'd had the equivalent of Homer or Dante in English with a purely mystical theme, which could also be read psychologically? That is – the fall of mankind, from Wholeness into fragments, caused by reason and ego, then the rise back to Wholeness through art? The clash of the mechanistic and the spiritual?

Our problem with Blake begins and ends with his over-blown home-made mythology, the product of an isolated and introverted mind, no doubt. The characters are all there, particularly Blake's hero, Los (Sol or Light), like a god of Creativity. Los is also a blacksmith who builds a City of Poetry (called Golgonooza) in Ulro, the wasteland of ice and frost created by Urizen (Reason). In one epic, *The First Book of Urizen,* Reason brings about the Fall when he splits off from the wholeness of Eternity. Until then, we'd all been a steady-state

67

mix of four well-balanced forces: emotion, creativity, energy, and reason. Urizen can't see that without 'contraries' there can be no life – you can't have joy without pain, love unbalanced by hate. Instead, Urizen writes laws in his brass-bound book forbidding unhappiness, strife, and hate. He makes it illegal *not* to feel pity or compassion. So Eternity threw the fool out, and then of course Eternity collapsed since the Whole needs all of its parts to be place and in balance.

Outside of Eternity, Reason is at first a shapeless mess of sulphur, pitch and saltpetre. Los shapes a body for him out of the chaos which Reason has, of course, just caused. Then, although he's been given the gift of a body, Reason, ungrateful as ever, makes a net of religion to catch, trap, snare and control us all.

In *Urizen* that lost unity is never restored. In *Milton* it is. A rough paraphrase could run like this: On earth Blake (a true poet and so a son of Creativity) is at loggerheads with Hayley (Blake's employer but also a bad poet and therefore Satan). Milton in Heaven gets wind of the quarrel and realises that he too, in his earthly days, had been Satanic – a true poet who'd betrayed the cause of Wholeness through narrow Puritanism. He comes back to earth – via Blake's big toe, for some reason – to make amends. Los, the spirit of Creativity, helps him. Milton also helps himself by re-absorbing his previously banished female half, Ololon. Between Los and Milton (and Blake) the Divine Vision once again enters the soul of fallen mankind and Wholeness is regained.

Jerusalem, the Emanation of the Giant Albion could have been the second great mystic epic for our times. Albion is all of us, each of us, and also England. He/we cause the Fall – the splintering of Eternal Wholeness into fragments through our rejection both of God's love and of our female side (here personified as Jerusalem) out of jealousy.

It's the job of Los to put it all together again, which in the end he does. For an epic, it's a bit plotless though there is the outline of one. For example, at the beginning Los has to outface his Spectre – our cold, over-rational, over-male, self-righteous and cruel side. Los dragoons him into helping to build the eternal city of art where all is 'Enameld with love & kindness'.

On the whole, *Jerusalem* (and the other would-be epics) reads like the work of an isolated, strong-willed, middle aged man obsessed with a private vision. Blake worked on *Jerusalem* throughout his fifties, financially one of the poorest decades of his seventy years. It's very old-fashioned – more 16th century than 19th, too steeped in an outmoded Hermetic Tradition and not enough in the Enlightenment. It's pre-Bacon, let alone pre-Newton. On the whole it's too overblown, too full of groaning, wailing and weeping, shouting, shaking and trembling.

Los tries to build a city of art with tiles of engraved gold and rafters of forgiveness, but sadly Blake had lost his gift for the bright phrase. Here's a sample taken at random: 'Albion,' cries Vala, 'thy fear has made me tremble: thy terror has surrounded me/Thy Sons have nailed me on the Gate piercing my hands and feet.'

Blake's early work has the greatness of simplicity based on deep ideas. Who doesn't know (the short) *Jerusalem* ('And was Jerusalem builded here,/Among these dark Satanic Mills?') or *Tyger, Tyger* ('burning bright/In the forests of the night')? An epic for our times should have been written in lines like these or else like Coleridge's *The Rime of the Ancient Mariner*. (Coleridge, incidentally, admired the early Blake not only as a poet but as a fellow-mystic also.)

CHAPTER TWELVE

The Garden of Love

Yet Blake had the right idea. Not only people but art should be a wholeness. To that end he wanted to make books like Medieval psalters: colour, pictures, poetry, calligraphy in a single whole.

We think of POD – Print-on-Demand – books as things of the computer age: warehouses stacked with rows of printers turning out half a million books a year. Nowadays, books can be printed in a bookshop – or airport, or coffee shop (or anywhere else) – on large copiers-cum-binders called Espresso Machines. Blake had a similar, though slow motion, idea over two hundred years ago (in 1788 or '89). His first problem – a technical one (where do you begin?) – was solved by the ghost of his brother, Robert, who by then had been dead for several months (you really do have to wonder if the man was quite right in the head). Anyway, the brotherly ghost put in an appearance and came up with the answer. Write the words and draw the pictures in an acid-proof liquid on a page-sized copper plate. Then pour on acid to eat away the unprotected bits to make a printing block. Print each page on a hand-press, then fill in the figures and background with paint.

A little later, St Joseph – presumably the Virgin Mary's Joseph – told him to use carpenter's glue to bind the colours. The colours he used read like poetry in themselves: indigo, cobalt, vermillion, ultra-marine, gamboge (a kind of yellow named, after Cambodia). Blake, and sometimes Mrs Blake, painted in the colours with a camel's hair, never a sable, brush.

His first Illuminated Books were *Songs of Innocence, The Book of Thel, The Marriage of Heaven and Hell* and *Songs of Experience.* It was technically and artistically a brilliantly successful idea. Sales were where it fell down – few bought it. For sheer mysticality, however, some of his earlier works are next door to near perfection.

Where Blake went wrong, I think, was with his home-made mythology – otherwise his ideas were fairly straightforward and orthodox, mystically speaking. They can be summarised (as we've already partly seen): each of us is pre-existently immortal but we know death because we're born into it: this world *is* death. Once here, we're manacled by Reason. We're killed by tyrants, kings, churches, parents, schoolmasters, childhood oppression, religion, social injustice. The 'dark Satanic mills' are the mills of Reason – of Bacon, Newton, Locke, science, the Enlightenment – and they grind us all exceeding small, creating 'tombstones where flowers should be'.

> In every cry of every Man,
> In every Infant's cry of fear,
> In every voice, in every ban,
> The mind-forg'd manacles I hear.

'Joy – delight – is the essence or life,' said Kathleen Raine, summing up, in fact, every mystic's insight, not just Blake's. 'The tigers of wrath are wiser than the horses of instruction' because the tiger is the true nature of things and the haltered and bridled horse has nothing to teach it – it can only twist nature out of its proper shape. 'Innocence' is life as it should be – full of joy in the light of eternity. 'Experience' is its opposite: life hindered and blocked by laws and reason, priests and schoolmasters ('the horses of instruction'.)

The Garden of Love is from *Songs of Experience*. The pages are tiny, little more than three inches by four and a half. The top third is filled with a picture in dark green, black and brown. A priest kneels at an open grave with a church wall and window behind him. His left palm is open – he's just flung a handful of earth onto the coffin in the grave. He reads from a book. Beside him kneel two fair haired children (a boy and a girl?), hands clasped in prayer, heads bowed either in grief or piety.

The words take up the bottom two thirds of the page. Each stanza is separated by a sinister, sinuous worm-like, snake-like, line. The garden, of course, represents innocence or the mystical ability to see eternity from whence we come, and whither we go. The priest represents experience – he's a duped and deluded, hapless destroyer of all that's good. Here is the poem in full:

I went to the Garden of Love,
And saw what I never had seen;
A Chapel was built in the midst,
Where I used to play on the green.

And the gates of this Chapel were shut
And 'Thou shalt not,' writ over the door;
So I turned to the Garden of Love
That so many sweet flowers bore.

And I saw it was filled with graves,
And tombstones where flowers should be;
And priests in black gowns were walking their rounds
And binding with briars my joys and desires.

Part Four

Personal

How do you illustrate minor mysticism and its undertones?
Throughout the summer of 2010, I wrote a blog mainly about
just such things. Some entries seem slight but that's the nature
of these experiences: they're brief but given importance by
their ubiquity. This, in fact, was the reason for a blog-like
approach – a deliberate attempt to catch these cursory
impressions as they came and went each day. If they're not
noted down, they evaporate very quickly.

Also, looking back, a good many of the film
documentaries I researched and wrote were about undertones,
one way or another. A good few of them too, I now note, were
in remote or out of the way (or just slightly off the beaten
track) places: crowds and undertones rarely mix.

CHAPTER THIRTEEN

On Location

Karl Weschke had a house on Cape Cornwall. His rented studio in St Ives opened on to a little sandy cove, except you couldn't see it because the windows were covered with translucent white paper to control the light. He was in his late sixties when we filmed him and he was looking forward to painting one more masterpiece. He'd had a strange life. His father – whom he met briefly and for the first time when he was eleven – died in Auschwitz. His mother was a part time prostitute. During the War he'd been a tail gunner with the Luftwaffe, but never in action until he joined a parachute regiment when he was wounded and taken prisoner by Commandos. As a hard line Nazi, he had to go through the de-Nazification programme which, for him, included an art course run by Cambridge University and a longish stay with a Quaker family in Saffron Walden. That was, he said, his first encounter with a civilised life and what it could offer.

John le Carré, a friend, spoke at the memorial service: 'Karl's was no easy journey. He never wanted it to be. No compromises, no evasions, no slick fabrications, no God. ... We do Karl no justice ... if we turn our eyes away from the chaos that made him. All his life, Karl wrestled with demons that most of us ... can only guess at – and having guessed would greatly prefer to look away.' Except of course there are no demons, only (pathology apart) deficiencies or incompletion, something which Weschke himself – judging solely from his work – proved by growing bigger than they were.

Weschke knew Francis Bacon and, at times, superficially resembles him but he was always his own man. I'd guess he was more genuine than Bacon, that tiresomely drunken habitué of

74

Soho's French Pub and Muriel's Colony Rooms. Was Weschke a mystic? Not in the least, but some of his best work is good enough to begin to act as triggers. In some, by no means all, of his paintings there is a kind of godless spirituality, an elemental power, a depiction of the way things are when nature has been subverted. In other words, they evoke desolation experiences.

His earlier vision was bitter. He got through a few women in his time but his drawings and paintings often show them naked and over-thrown like gladiators waiting for the thumbs down and the final sword thrust. Was that because of the mass rape of German women by the Red Army in 1945? *Europa and the Bull* (1988-9) is of a white animal hoof-deep in dark, shallow water against a brown sky. Europa, painted brown, lies full length, face down with legs apart, along the bull's back. Most of Weschke's human figures, in fact, are either naked and alive, or naked and dead and decayed, but always alone, floating in dark seas, or lonely on iron-bound shores, starkly white against dark seascapes. Savage looking dogs appear in empty landscapes, fighting or devouring meat. In some cases, describing his work invokes more of a feeling of desolation than you get from looking at them. Which is an indictment, I suppose.

Some of the 1980s landscapes do have a kind of sadness and repose. *Rainbow at Kenidjack* (1987-9) is of a dark sky, grey tinged with grey-blue, a grey sea, a black headland, and a rainbow curving like water poured from a spout. *Leda and the Swan* (1985-6) I think was still in his studio when we filmed. She stands thigh deep in a still grey-green sea with her back to the viewer and with her right hand reaching down behind her. (Weschke told us the postman caught him one morning with his trousers down trying to catch the exact pose he wanted.) She looks down menacingly at Zeus, the top god, in the guise of a swan who, meek and timorous, gazes up at her. Behind then are brown cliffs like a palisade of logs. Two great brown trees grow on an unseen beach or perhaps in the sea itself. It's a half-undertone kind of painting.

His colours, and his mind, lightened with age. As he got older, he turned to the sunshine of Egypt. The pyramid at *Giza* (1994) is an abstraction of triangles: orange-terracotta coloured pyramid with triangular mauve-blue skies on either side. *The Nile at Kom Ombo* – painted in the same year – is almost an abstraction of three horizontals: light sandy brown land, dark blue river, lighter blue sky.

From time to time, when researching a film, I asked people in the arts if what they did was at all mystical: none said it was. Before I met him I was pretty sure Colin Baxter's photographs were, but he too said no. He began, as I understood, by making postcards out of pictures he'd taken of Scottish landscapes and hawking them around hotels for sale to tourists. When we filmed him, he had a big house below the Cairngorms and his own company to publish his own books, with a warehouse to store them in.

Most of his pictures are of a Scotland rarely seen. Some are more lush than that country really is. Others are of places so remote that few go there. And all are rare because the light in Scotland can change by the minute so you never see the same scene twice. To get shots like Baxter's you have to wait for days on end, always ready to shoot when the light is right. His books are full of extraordinary pictures of ice-scoured, ice-scarred glens and ice-scraped peaks, massive upheavals of rock bare save for fields of snow. Sharp stacs rise sheer from the sea with the sky above dusted with birds – so many that at first you think the camera lens needed cleaning.

Some of his landscapes are richly romantic and alluring. Colour, as we've seen, can be adamic on its own and the colours in his shot of the road to Glenelg, for example, is a case in point. A thin thread of a line of a road runs, barely visible, down a great green hillside. You'd think it should lead to Shangri-La rather than, as it does, to an ordinary village on the shore. Above all this greenness, the normally sharp-edged, cinder-grey Cuillins rise up soft and pink under the yellow sky of a fading western day.

Gavin Maxwell shared a cottage with his otters a little farther along the coast from Glenelg and wrote, I think, *A Ring of Bright Water* there. The title is from a poem by Kathleen Raine, who was a mystic and a Platonist and who lived there for a time in unrequited love for Maxwell. He'd gone to that remote place looking for peace before the War ended, having been invalided out of the Scots Guard. His last Army job had been to clear up a bomb shelter in London after either a doodlebug or a V2 had hit it. The place was awash with urine, excreta, blood and body parts. Even now you can imagine the contrast between blitzed London and this clean shore across the Sound of Sleight from the Isle of Skye and the razor-like Cuillin Mountains, with blue headland beyond blue headland fading out into the Western sea.

Most of Baxter's photographs, on the other hand, are a reminder that Scotland is a place of water as much as mountain. Most of his pictures, if not of the sea, are filled with lochs and lochans, rivers, salt marsh, pools or bogs. Water and ice sculpted that landscape. But water can also *be* sculpted.

In fact, we once filmed a whole building which was, in effect, a water sculpture. It was the British Pavilion in Seville at the Expo there in '92. The building, little more than an oblong box of glass, was by Nicholas Grimshaw: William Pye was the sculptor. You could, I suppose, call what he'd made a kind of painting, with water and light replacing paint and canvas. The front wall of the building was some two hundred and fifty feet long by forty high: ten thousand square feet of glass down which water poured in controlled waves: wavelets, really, or – better still – glinting scribbles of water and light. More prosaically, you could think of it as a double glazing of glass and water which gleamed, glittered, sparkled, changed and glinted until the Spanish sun went down.

Sunlight and water are individually good for undertones: combined, they work perfectly, particularly as the wave wall ended in a water fall which cascaded noisily into a moat. To get into the building, you walked behind this colonnade-like fall of water, cooling the hot Seville sun.

Sculpting water was Pye's speciality: he first got the idea while walking up a tarmac'd road in a storm in Wales: rain water ran down the road in curiously fixed wave patterns, always the same, always changing. But behind the sculptures, making them work, was some pretty hard mathematics. The water flow in Seville was computer controlled but with other works the controlling factor is geometry. We filmed, for example,

Jetstream and *Slipstream* in Gatwick airport. They're tilted cones down which water flows in fixed but ever-changing waves controlled entirely by the geometry, the shape, of the metal structures.

That sculpture in Seville was a stand-alone but, meanwhile, in the darker, damper north, the commercial forest of Grizedale in Cumbria also doubled up as an art gallery. Each year a new artist was asked to make a sculpture to place among the trees. The proviso was that it should either rot back into the soil or fit in and weather like a dry stone wall. Most were therefore made of wood. Some were over-conceptual: one lad hung real wooden chairs in trees, for example: there was a conceptual reason for doing so, but I've forgotten it. Another was an arch carved with insects crawling from the earth on one side, over the keystone, and down into the earth on the other side. Again, that was a bit obvious – and an odd choice since the sculptor didn't know how to carve and had never been taught about sculpture in art school.

Unsurprisingly, Andy Goldsworthy's work was best. *Seven Spires* was a tall slender steeple of bare trunks leaning together in a forest clearing, in the scent of pines. The religious overtones were as loud as the spiritual undertones were muted. His *Taking a Wall for a Walk* didn't work so well. A dry stone wall wound and looped (come to think of it, it probably still does) around the boles of single trees as though they, and not the wall, are what matter. It just looks a bit too much like a thought.

Ting, very unusually, wasn't made of wood or stone: it was an enormous steel ring resting on the ground but also looped through the high branches of a deciduous tree in a paddock-like field. *The Axis of the Earth,* by Masao Ueno, was a ball or globe of slender coppiced branches with a stick (the axis) rising through the North Pole. The rod-like branches were laid like lines of latitude but tilted diagonally, south to north. It was nicely placed, as well, on top of a fern-covered rise, letting the sky and rare sun shine through.

The Eye was an egg-shaped heap of stones of the kind used in dry walling. It looked more like a fir cone than an egg, more like egg than an eye, but right for the forest. *Marimba* was a kind of xylophone with half a dozen differently pitched planks of timber hanging in a little alcove of stone. It was playable, after a fashion, but whether or not you could play a tune on it, I don't know. The cone/egg/eye, the spires and the globe were the undertone-makers, turning a secular, damp, commercial forest into something almost mystical.

Most forests, of course, can be mystical without having to have works of art dotted all through them. Not all, though. Something more than standing timber is sometimes needed and that something, I suspect, is an emotional connection. The rainforest of Korup in Cameroon carried no undertones for me at all. Apart from the heat and humidity, it looked not unlike an English wood of slender trees, but with no primroses around the margins. The mangrove swamp at the mouth of the Korup River was better for undertones but that may have been because of associations with the open sea. We landed at the village at the head of a creek in pitch darkness: the boatman had forgotten the river was tidal, so we had to lie off waiting for the flood. Undrilled soldiers interrogated us in the hot darkness under harsh hanging light bulbs. Most of the rest of the night was then spent making speeches and haggling with the village elders over the fees. We filmed, in the daylight, the dance of the Leopard Spirit Cult.

Perhaps not so strangely, the strongest undertones were aroused by a graveyard of steam boats beached at a bend in the river, forlornly rusted and pocked by shell fire. They were almost certainly built on the Clyde or Tyne in the later years of Queen Victoria. For some, that too carries its own undertones.

Something similar was true of Romania. Tulcea is the last town before the great reed marsh through which the Danube filters into the Black Sea. The Romanian Navy – this was not long after the Cold War – had several old gun boats tied up there. One in particular had a huge after deck which must have carried a big gun in her Victorian or Edwardian hey day.

The reed marsh is astonishing – hundreds of square miles of tall reeds which you can see neither through nor over. Except in the open waterways, visibility is measured in inches and the rustling of the reeds is a constant five or six decibels. Run-away or renegade Russians lived and inbred there, surviving on fishing and wild boar hunting in the winter when the river and all the waterways freeze solid as roads.

At the mouth of the Danube is the village of Sfintu Gheorgu (St George) with beautifully carved wooden houses and soft, ankle-turning sand roads. The mayor was an ex-Party member (you could tell them by their paunches and brief cases) and completely tongue tied in front of the camera because, I imagine, he had no party line to follow. The place in fact was run by women, not only the village but also its main source of income – a caviar cannery across the river.

Jason sailed along this coast in *Argo,* with her sighted painted eyes, to Colchis and the Golden Fleece and the terrible revenge of Medea who he picked up there. Ovid wrote *Metamorphoses* or the *Book of Changes* when Augustus exiled him down that way. A later Roman Emperor, Marcus Aurelius, fought the barbarians in the reeds, sustained by his faith in Stoicism, a philosophy which Pope's *An Essay on Man* sums up quite nicely: 'All are but part of one stupendous whole,/Whose body, Nature is, and God the Soul.' It's strange how Stoicism had incorporated mystic insights without being mystical itself. It was partly derived, of course, from Heraclitus who thought that the unity underlying the cosmos was attenuated fire, not unlike (perhaps) our modern energy.

The sequences we shot in the Danube marshes were for a documentary about wetlands which also included the Norfolk Broads (those flooded Medieval peat diggings) and the Somerset Levels where the peat cuttings are pitch-black, hot and humid. It was our second visit to the Levels: the first had been to film a story about archaeology and, in particular, the newly discovered Sweet Track – named after Mr Sweet, the driver of the peat cutting machine which uncovered it. It was a strange, cut off landscape framed on three sides by beautiful low hills and on the fourth by the sea. Prehistorically it had been waterlogged but dotted with small islands of higher ground where people lived. The Sweet Track was just one of a network of planked wooden paths, raised above the water on stakes, which led from island to island.

More recently, houses on the Levels were two-storeyed to cope with the winter floods: boats were moored to the upper windows which acted as doors until the water went down again in summer. Jacquetta Hawkes also felt the mystic tug of time in this strange place. Somerset means Summer Settlers because it was settled only seasonally by the West Saxons. King Alfred is said to burned the cakes somewhere down there before his great battle against the Danes at Ethandune in Wiltshire, commemorated centuries later by G K Chesteron in *The Ballad of the White Horse* (although he got the location wrong, siting the battle in the Vale of the White Horse in what is now Oxfordshire).

Even Thomas Hardy, that most unmystical of men, was inspired by an event which took place on the Polden Hills, the western frame of the Levels. In his 1902 ballad, *The Trampwoman's Tragedy,* he retold a true story from the 1850s. Two tramping couples stopped to drink ale in an inn on the crest of the Poldens: Mother Lee and Jeering Johnny were now together after swapping partners with the heroine-narrator and her new fancy man (both unnamed). The narrator teases her fancy man by telling him Jeering Johnny is the father of the child's she's carrying. The fancy man stabs Jeering Johnny to death and is duly hanged. Mother Lee dies at Glastonbury and the narrator miscarries. As she lies in the open all alone, the ghost of her fancy man appears. She assures him he was the father of their now dead child.

Pretty typical Hardy you might think, except it's lifted by something extra. Three stanzas might make the point:

Full twenty miles we jaunted on,

   ....

My fancy-man, and jeering John,
And Mother Lee, and I.
And, as the sun drew down to west,
We climbed the toilsome Polden crest,
And saw, of landskip sights the best,
The inn that beamed thereby.

Lone inns we loved, my man and I,
....
'King's Stag', 'Windwhistle' high and dry,
'The Horse' on Hintock Green,
The cosy house at Wynyard's Gap,
'The Hut', renowned on Bredy Knap,
And many another wayside tap
Where folk might sit unseen.

Thus Polden top at last we won,
......
And gained the inn at sink of sun
Far-famed as 'Marshal's Elm'.
Beneath us figured tor and lea,
From Mendip to the western sea
I doubt if any finer sight there be
Within this royal realm.

Undertones? In continuity, the sadness and repose of place, pity for human nature, sadness for past time as epitomised in the list of inns, and the occasional euphony of the words.

Across the county border in Dorset, the Purbeck Hills are another near perfect range – easily encompassable and with views of the sea. The ruins of Corfe Castle gauntly fill a gap in the green hills. We went there to film an ecological riddle. The Adonis Blue butterfly lives on the hills at the very northerly edge of its range. It can live there, in fact, only because the Purbecks are in the far south of England and are also south facing. For centuries the hills had been part of a single estate before being bequeathed to the National Trust. There was no pollution, no pesticides, in fact no farming at all, and yet the Adonis Blue was dying out. Why?

To solve the puzzle, the butterfly's whole life cycle was analysed. In the chrysalis stage it's cared for, symbiotically, by a species of ant. The ants tend it, keep it clean and free of predators. In return, they're given sugar on mushroom shaped glands which sprout, like fungi, when the back of the chrysalis is stroked.

The ultimate cause the decline, it turned out, was the absence of sheep. For centuries, until the price of wool dropped, sheep had grazed the hills. Without the sheep, the grass grew longer and the long grass changed the micro-climate on the surface of the soil. The temperature, in fact, dropped a full degree centigrade and that was the immediate cause of the decline. But there's a twist to the story. The slight heat loss didn't effect the Adonis Blue, only the ants which looked after it. The ants too are at the northern limit of their range and can't cope with even such a small loss of warmth. The butterfly, in fact, was in decline solely because it was no longer being cared for. The answer, then, was simple: put sheep back on the hills. The undertones were generated by place, continuity, and the butterfly's strange story.

Acrophobia, or fear of heights, isn't something you expect in either the Poldens or the Purbecks. Just as well because fear generated by height carries no undertones. Once we filmed from the roof of a tower block in Manchester. In fact, two tower blocks joined at the top by ducting which we had to cross to film the right side of the city. The ducting was L-shaped with one half forming a wall: on the other side was a rail-less drop to the street below. Nor were there rails around the roof of the buildings proper. Stupidly, I crossed, but stayed only until I could no longer stand the sight of the cameraman's shoes, with his feet inside, sticking out over the abyss. As I retreated in defeat, I left a line of wet hand prints on top of the raised ducting. Even in that craven state I looked back at them in astonishment: how could a human palm leak so much water? Steep stairs took you down to the lifts, and then an endless journey down the shaft thinking all the while that only an inch or two of flooring lay between you and the oily bottom of the pit.

I never usually get that sensation on mountains or very steep slopes probably because you can save yourself, if only by crawling. It was odd, then, to get it in the middle of a mountain – in the unfinished turbine hall of the hydro-electric station at Dinorwic in Wales. Half the mountain had already been hollowed out into an enormous straight-walled, squared-off cavern: the drop below the shelf, which was to house the control room, fell away into the darkness below. It was railed, but a rail is never enough for people who have a fear of heights.

83

Desolation undertones were another matter: they were there in that vast hollow mountain and also on the summit in the outdoors high above. It was mid-winter and we stood at the same height as the higher peaks of rock, ice and snow. (A peakscape? The acrosphere?) There's a lake on top where a unique species of Arctic Chub had evolved after the end of the Ice Age. They're not there now because, at times of high demand for electricity, the plug is pulled and most of the lake cascades down through shafts in the rock into the turbines and then down into a lake at the foot of the mountain.

The granite quarry at Glensanda overlooking Loch Linnhe in Scotland is an equally bold bit of engineering. In contrast, we shot it in perfect (but unlikely) Highland weather in midsummer. It's a strangely out-of-sight kind of quarry. Instead of slicing away the side of a mountain, the centre is being taken out, after the manner of an apple-corer. Yeoman, the quarriers, sank a vertical shaft from summit to sea level. Stone is quarried in a circle around this Glory Hole, and bulldozed into it. Gravity takes the granite down to the sea. Conveyor belts then carry it to crushing, grading and storing sheds. From there it's loaded into supertanker-sized ships at a barely visible wharf. Even though the quarry wasn't fully working, rock was already being shipped to Kent to be made into liners for the Channel Tunnel.

The West Highland coast was quite an undertone-generating place in those days. As, oddly, are massive engineering works. There's a sense of sinking into a greater wholeness in mountain landscapes, and also in being enveloped inside great hills, as you are in adit mines. There were two of them on that coast back then. The barytes mine at Strontian (hence strontium) was adamic in a small way. Not as strongly though as the 'pillar and stall' silica mine above Loch Aline on the Morvern Peninsula. Pillars of sand were left untouched to hold up the roof: silica was quarried in smaller 'stalls', like rooms or chambers. It was quite warm inside the mine and the sand was pure white. All in all, it was like being buried in a mountain of unthawable hot snow. Hard walking it was, too, over the soft floor, as bad as the unpaved streets of Sfintu Georghu. In worked-out places, you stood in a silence, stillness and whiteness of Hammershøi-an intensity. Elsewhere, enormous dumper trucks roared down the tunnels, headlights blazing. Outside in the open air, they shot sand down chutes into coast-going ships moored to the jetty a long way below.

The mine had opened only in the early days of the War when high quality glass was needed for bomb sights and binoculars. Until then it had come from Germany. The mine's shut now.

The place was strangely redolent of the War years: you could sense both wartime peacefulness and the war's closeness because the loch opened out into the Atlantic where U-Boats, corvettes and convoys fought. The wrecks of torpedoed ships are still there and visitable. I remember diving on one called the *Buitenzorg* somewhere near the Isle of Mull. She'd been torpedoed in 1941 and had turned turtle on her way down. At first, I couldn't see a wreck at all. Then I realised that the strangely smooth rock over which I was swimming was, in fact, her up-turned hull and keel, only a five or six feet proud of the sea bed, covered all over with pale Dead Men's Fingers.

More spectacular was the wreck of the *Tapti*, one of a line of small steamers named after Indian rivers. She'd been torpedoed at anchor close to the island of either Tiree or Col in the Inner Hebrides. Her wheel and binnacle were still intact on the bridge, all canted over to starboard. The wheel, covered with sea anemones, was like a floral clock. Portuguese Men o' War drifted by trailing long stings in the bright, sunlit water. The only sounds were the intermittent roar of my escaping air and the dive boat's engine tock-tocking in the sea-sky. Some verses, written twenty-five or so years later, underline the lasting strength of the undertones that kind of thing can generate.

> The ship was newly coaled
> To be torpedoed as she rode
> At anchor here.
>
> Her wheel was a floral clock
> Of gold and mauve anemones
> Swaying in a breeze of tide.
> Tock-tock of diesel in the sky.
> You grew quite fond

Of rubbery kelp and fronds
Of bladder wrack and weed,
But, scubaman, you can't live there,
An alien with your bottled air.

Sun began to sink.
Mull was mauve. Then pink.
You licked your lenses free
And peered through spindrift and the sea.
(The Moon at Midnight)

More peacefully, and finally, *Patricia* was a replica Victorian steamboat, all brass, copper, coal, elegance and iron fitted into a GRP or fibre glass hull. She was built, I think, at Bossom's Boatyard way up the river opposite Oxford. Manley Hopkins's Binsey poplars were just along the bank. *The Scholar Gipsy's* Bablock Hythe is a mile or so farther upstream.

Patricia had quite a tall funnel (and, of course, a steam whistle) and a little glass encased saloon for wide-frocked Victorian ladies. There was a very small stoke hole where the stoker-cum-engineer-cum-steersman could shovel in coal by the pound, or ounce. The undertones were from steam, continuity and messing about in boats although we were quite a way upstream from *The Wind in the Willows*. The world of just-before-you-were-born seems young, not old, and there was an ancient innocence about that replica Victorian pleasure boat.

CHAPTER FOURTEEN

Day by Day

1 Inner Space

Jacques Cousteau's demand valve might seem an odd aid to the lesser mysticism, but so it can be. (It's the device which makes scuba-diving possible by delivering air to the lungs at the same pressure as the surrounding water.) Being able to move three-dimensionally in another world can be a serious undertone-inducing experience. Shoals of fish stand in for flocks of flying birds, and upright kelp can be like a forest of swaying trees. In clear weather, you fly through shafts of watery sunlight below the ceiling of the under-surface of the sea.

Diving on a wreck can add a human side – if, that is, the ship is reasonably intact. The Cunarder *Aurania*, for example, was torpedoed in 1918 in Calgary Bay, off the Isle of Mull. Sixty years after her sinking she was just a vast flattened mass of hull plates, pipes and girders, home to a four foot long fish. She lies under the black and craggy rocks of Caliak Point, perennially chilled by the sea. Low water exposes a cave. Any mystic moment there is of the desolation kind.

In contrast, in the summer of 1970, the *Glen Strathalan* was scuttled just outside Plymouth breakwater. She'd heeled over slightly to port but still sat upright on the sea bed. It was a strange experience – she seemed alive yet ghostly, eerie, as she rode the bottom of the sea. The paint work was still uncorroded but already weed was beginning to grow on rails and funnel which almost broke the surface fifty feet above her keel. The wheelhouse and all the superstructure were intact and you could swim on-board.

87

The isosceles shaped Mewstone is close by, grey-rocked but green-peaked. In those days you could land, for a picnic lunch if for nothing else. A convict had been transported there in the 1740s (with his family, oddly enough) and then, in the early 19th century, a warrener (and family) lived on the rock. The ruins of the little circular house must have been theirs. You can see the mouth of the River Yealm (pronounced 'yam') from there but not the old fishing villages of Newton Ferrers and Noss Mayo in a narrow, timbered valley where blue mullet came to the head of the creek on the flood tide. That summer, green trees came down to the water's edge, like skirts. You cross a harbour bar to gain the open sea, which is all very Tennysonesque *. All of it was a place of unadulterated undertones in those far off days.

*He rose at dawn and, fired with hope,
Shot o'er the seething harbour-bar,
And reach'd the ship and caught the rope,
And whistled to the morning star.

2 'A Sensitivity to Mysticism'

Where Stace went wrong, I think, was in being too dismissive of lower levels of mysticism. He stuck a bit too closely to the extreme end of the spectrum. Nature mysticism he dismissed as 'a dim feeling or sense of a 'presence' in nature which does not amount to a developed mystical experience but is a kind of sensitivity to the mystical which many people have who are not in the full sense mystics'.

Stace goes on to say that Wordsworth was probably not a mystic. Sensitive people, he writes, pick up ideas and delude themselves that they sense things more than they do. Yet nothing at all about Wordsworth suggests this is true. For one thing, he lost his mystic sight at around the age of thirty-five although the bulk of his work was written after that. If he'd been working only with second hand ideas, why did he stop?

88

His *Ecclesiastic Sonnets* are little more than a history of the church since 597, and in pretty poor verse at that. Underhill, in contrast, goes too far the other way: she'd have called anybody a mystic who merely thought there was something in it. That may be a step too far but, all the same, Stace's caution is worth bearing in mind.

3 The Light of Eternity

In his book, *Mysticism, Christian and Buddhist,* Suzuki wrote: 'I have been reading all day, confined to my room, and feel tired. I raise the screen and face the broad daylight. I move the chair on the verandah and look at the blue mountains. I draw a deep breath, fill my lungs with fresh air and feel entirely refreshed. I make tea and drink a cup or two. Who would say that I am not living in the light of eternity?' Very few would say he was, is probably today's correct answer. And yet I've come to think that this lesser, extrovertive, undertone-like kind of mysticism is best: always on tap, demotic, and with no need of *zazen,* rosaries or a saintly life-style.

4 James Summed Up

What was William James's own summing up of his findings? That this world is incomplete on its own because it's only a part of a greater, spiritual whole which gives it meaning: that the spiritual is reachable: that reaching it releases energy which can materially and psychologically change people and things. You can call it either God or Law.

Although we can rarely know the truth about anything, he added, we *can* tell whether something works or not. If it does, it has a 'cash value' – that is, it's valuable in a practical sense. It is, in fact, a kind of working truth. There's no evidence, for example, that God exists. You can either believe, disbelieve or say you don't know. But saying you don't know has the same practical outcome as disbelief. Benefits which might accrue to you are lost.

(I say 'a kind of working truth' to skirt the pitfall of the Pragmatic Fallacy – the belief that if something works it must be true.)

5 James's Conclusion

In the end, William James, although no mystic himself, came around to thinking that there *was* something in it. People who had apex-of-the-soul experiences generally thought they were genuine. Be more open minded, he told the doubters – mystics just might be right. He took his own advice, in line with his Pragmatist philosophy which says that whatever works is a kind of truth. Whatever mysticism is, it is an experience – that is, something real in its own way – with life-completing power. Discarding it would be folly.

Henri Bergson also told people to accept what the mystics say. Esoteric and exoteric weren't words he used (as far as I know, and that isn't very far) but that's what he meant. Exoteric religion is static and repressive and leads to a closed society. Esoteric spirituality is liberating, open and dynamic. Few people can be Grade One mystical types but most can get some idea of what it's all about and should opt for freedom and the open mind.

6 Belief Strengthens Belief

More controversially, James also said that the act of believing makes the belief not just stronger (in you) but more true. Does belief in National Socialism or Communism bear that out? They're certainly very adhesive in affected minds but perhaps we should add: an idea is untrue if it's an outlet for your own spleen and resentment, and thus diminishes you or damages others. Any belief which ends in gas chambers or gulags is based on false premises and fails the 'does this make us bigger and better?' test. James's Radical Empiricism lets you believe in God if – and only if – that belief increases and expands you.

People have gained from these ideas. A woman wrote to Hardy in the 1970s: 'About ten years later I began to pray for my children's safety, and this became a habit which I have never lost, and often the answer to such a prayer is spectacular. Now I've evolved a belief which is identical with Beatrice Webb's: 'I find it best to live as if the soul of man were in communion with a superhuman force which makes for righteousness' ... May I add that since this belief grew in me I feel as if I had grown, as if my mind had stretched to take in the vast universe and be part of it. (Which seems to bear out William James's contention that belief strengthens belief.)'

7 James on 'Stuff'

Two or three of William James's other ideas are also important to mysticism, even if a bit obliquely. The basic idea of his Radical Empiricism, as I understand it, says that we can't know anything objectively because mind and matter are the same thing, aspects of an unbroken wholeness. We are like surf on the sea. He called it neutral monism. The cosmos is based on a single 'stuff': mind is one way of organising this stuff, matter is another. Both at bottom are the same. Religious experiences, James argued, 'point with reasonable probability' to there being only one Consciousness of which the human kind is a small part.

8 Bohr

Niels Bohr pointed out in the 1920s that some questions can't be asked because they have no answer. The only question you can ask of anything in nature is: What is it doing now? How is it behaving? One example sometimes given concerns colour. Blue is blue in sunlight, black by lamplight. Blood is red in daylight, black to a scuba diver below five fathoms. Which is right? Wrong question: How does blue behave in this light? is the right one. And, how does red behave in light-filtering sea water? Another example is the sub-atomic particle. Is it bullet-like or wave-like? Wrong question again because there can be no answer, not at the present evolutionary level of our brains.

So the best question you can ask of mysticism is: what does it do? The answer is: quite a lot.

9   Where Have All the Mystics Gone?

One of the strangest things about the 19th century West was the sheer number of artistic mystics and scientists who lived either wholly or partly between 1801-1901. I make it getting on for a hundred:

AE, Baudelaire, Berenson, Blake, Bradley, Brancusi, Robert Bridges (?)Emily Brontë, Rupert Brooke, Brown, Mr and Mrs Browning, Buchan, Richard Bucke, Carlyle, Chapman, G K Chesterton, S T Coleridge, Teilhard de Chardin, Emily Dickinson, Dostoyevsky, Einstein, Emerson, Fichte, Foucauld, Galgani, Garrigou-Lagrange, Gissing, Gödel, Grou, Hammarskjöld, Hammershøi (?), F C Happold, Alister Hardy, Hegel, Hölderlin, Holst, Hopkins, Hügel, Jefferies, Karl Joel, Jung, Kandinsky, Keats, Kingsley, Lucie-Christine, Mallarmé, Masefield, Henry Martyn, Messiaen, Mondrian, Montague, Cardinal Newman, Robert Nichols, Ben Nicholson (?), Novalis, Palmer, Coventry Patmore, Peladan, Ruth Pitter, J C and F T Powys, Proust, Raine, Rilke, Rimbaud, D G and C Rossetti, J W Rowntree, Ruskin, Satie, Schleiemacher, Shelley, Schopenhauer, Scriabin, Soloviev, Steiner, Tennyson, Therese, Thompson, Thoreau, Tolstoy, Trevelyan, Unamuno, Evelyn Underhill, Varese, Leslie Weatherhead, Beatrice Webb, Weil, Whitman, Charles Williams, Vaughan Williams, Wittgenstein, Virginia Woolf (?), Wordsworth.

Possibles include: Eddington, Heisenberg, Jeans, Henry Moore, Pauli, Schrödinger, Whitehead.

Doubtful ones proposed by Marghanita Laski: William Morris and even (surely not?) H G Wells. Others she proposed include: George Eliot, E M Forster, D H Lawrence, George Meredith.

Jacquetta Hawkes was an Edwardian, and so isn't counted. So was Cecil Collins, the painter. Arthur Koestler was born in 1905. Laski includes Carlo Levi (born 1902).

Wanted-to-bes: T S Eliot, Aldous Huxley.

Why were there so many? Why so few now?

10 Hawkes, Moore, Sculpture

Henry Moore didn't write much but, somewhere in his written work, he talks about the differences between Greek art and his own. The Greeks wanted statues to please the senses: he aimed at a deeper 'spiritual vitality'. By spiritual did he mean mystical? Jacquetta Hawkes, archaeologist, anthropologist, mystic and friend of Moore, saw a great deal more in his work than most people do, thereby nicely illustrating the enrichment which a mystical temperament brings. In her book, *A Land*, she compares Moore to Rodin. 'Rodin pursued the idea of conscious spiritual man emerging from the rock; Moore sees him rather as always a part of it.'

Moore was right, too, she thought, to use native stone and not imported Tuscan marble ('white silence,' as she called it). She particularly liked his choice of two-toned Hornton stone from the Jurassic Lias beds of Oxfordshire which are rich in fossils. Its colours are either light brown or green, the results of ancient climate change (so even the weather's solidified in stone). Moore used the greens for dark ideas, the browns for lighter ones, thus obeying a primeval instinct to choose dark colours for dark moods, light for light, derived from the primordial cycle of night and day.

What Jacquetta Hawkes experienced, I suspect, were continuity ecstasies: a sense of eternity brought on by an unbroken connection to ancient time. 'It is hardly possible,' she wrote, 'to express in prose the extraordinary awareness of the unity of the past and present, of mind and matter, of man and man's origin ... Once when I was in Moore's studio and saw one of his reclining figures with the shaft of a belemnite exposed in the thigh, my vision of this unity was overwhelming. I felt that the squid ... even while it still swam in distant seas was involved in this encounter with the sculptor.'

As we've seen, Pugin, Ruskin and Blake all thought the intellectuality of Renaissance-Greek architecture was wrong for churches and cathedrals. Only Gothic would do. Hawkes adds to the argument: 'Anyone who enters a Gothic cathedral must be aware that he is walking back into the primeval forest of existence, with birds, beasts, monsters and angels looking through the foliage. But with classical building man was giving expression to that upper part of his consciousness which would cut itself off more and more from its background to live in the Ionic temple of the intellect.' Moore, she concludes, reached deep into the stone to bring to the surface the life he found there.

There's a fair example of Moore's work – *Two Piece Reclining Figure No 5* (*1963-4*) – in the grounds of Kenwood House in the Hampstead Hills in north London. It's high on the slope overlooking the Thousand Guinea Lake. One part of the figure is a far from reclining rabbit with one bronze ear. It's comical and distracts from the impact of the whole. All the same, even if it doesn't evacuate the mind to let in spiritual sunlight, you can see what Moore was getting at, mystically speaking.

11   Zen of Stone

Stone can evoke the spiritual whether shaped by hand or by nature and the weather. Stone has texture but is mystical to the eye rather than the touch. It can be sculpted, of course but whatever is spiritual about it then mostly resides in the art, less so in the material. If the sculpture is poor, the stone's mystic-making ability is reduced and it should have been left in the quarry.

Similarly with stone in old buildings – it can have a spiritual quality, not because of its stoneness but, more usually, because of a sense of time stretched so far it's become timeless. And the timeless, as we know, is eternity and eternity is just another name for the mystic moment.

Sedimentary rocks are better, mystically speaking, than igneous. Possibly – probably – that has to do with the rougher friability of the stone. You can also imagine rock being slowly laid down, as quartz or coccoliths, on the bed of some warm, clear, sun-flickering sea with light filtering down past coelacanths, having already lit the leather wings of pterodactyls gliding in the hot air above. Igneous stone is all fire and violence. Granite and marble come into their own mainly as artefacts, not so much in their natural state.

Baked clay works mystically when it's rough, red, weathered and made into a wall. Machine made yellow and (worse) mauve coloured bricks don't work at all. An old – 17th or 18th century – brick wall is probably better than a stone one, though an individual piece of stone is more evocative than a single brick, even the bright red Roman kind. (Not that there was anything mystical about Rome – all those logically straight roads and logical Latin grammar, perhaps.)

12 Monkeying with Physics

The early 21st century came out in a rash of books by religious scientists. Arthur Peacocke (physical biochemist) wrote *Paths from Science towards God* and *Theology for a Scientific Age.* Ian Barbour (physicist) had: *Religion and Science* and *When Science Meets Religion.* Russell Stannard (physicist) edited *God for the 21st Century.* Alister McGrath (molecular biophysicist) wrote *The Dawkins Delusion.* Above all, John Polkinghorne (quantum physicist and priest) wrote or had already written: *Science and Theology*: *One World*: *Quarks, Chaos and Christianity*: *Reason and Reality*: *Traffic in Truth*: *Belief in God in an Age of Science.* Even non-scientists such as Keith Ward, a theologian, wrote about science and religion: *God, Faith and the New Millennium* which followed on from *God, Chance and Necessity.* From a bit earlier we have Gerald Schroeder's *The Science of God,* Nevill Mott's *Can Scientists Believe?* and Paul Davies's *The Mind of God.* (And they are only part of a long list.)

All, of course, are written from a rational point of view – it'd be surprising if they weren't. One of Peacocke's books, for instance, revolves around IBE (the Inference to Best Explanation) which argues that some kind of uncreated Creator best explains why the cosmos is as it is. Many other writers refer to the 'fine-tuning' of the mathematics governing the working of this particular universe. They're so precise that the universe was given no choice but to evolve conscious creatures. The level of accuracy of the maths has been compared (by Paul Davies, I think) to firing a bullet from one edge of the cosmos and hitting the bull's eye of a standard sized target on the other. Fire more bullets and they'd all land in the same square inch – across billions of light years of space.

From this level of improbable precision, some people argue for the existence of a God. It proves no such thing, of course, but to get around the embarrassment other scientists suggest there's an infinity of universes one of which was bound to get the maths right. I understand there is some kind of back up to this theory but, unless it can be proved, why bother? There's little comfort in an endless stream of dead and crippled cosmoi. Occam's Razor suggests that a God is a better answer. At any rate, for some scientists that fine tuning is the trump card.

It's called the *Anthropic Principle*. The phrase dates from the 1970s but the realisation that something strange is going on pre-dates it by at least sixty years. Fred Hoyle, an astrophysicist (and cosmologist), began as an atheist. In the post-War 1940s, he puzzled over the ratio of elements that go to make up the world, and us. He had the (correct) idea that the elements are made deep inside failing stars. At first, his problem was with carbon. With the figures he had at the time, carbon should break down before it can be useful. Later experiments showed that it had its own 'stabilising energy levels in its nucleus'. Hoyle ended his days as a theist, arguing that the universe is 'a put up job' and that 'a superintellect has monkeyed with physics'.

There's often something strained about science being used to defend exoteric religion. Many believing scientists, it's probably fair to say, tend towards a psychosomatic way of looking at the human mind/body/soul conundrum. Plato and Descartes are left far behind. Polkinghorne, for instance, believes that the information needed to re-create each of us is stored in God's mind. Come Doomsday, He'll reconstitute us all as psychosomatic creatures once again. (St Paul thought the same way – although, of course, without the Information Theory bit.) On the face of it, that sounds like bad news for the ill-favoured and otherwise imperfect – most of us, in fact. Needless to say, it's unmystical as well.

Most of these ideas can be convincing, but only if you want to be convinced in the first place: they give reasons for rejecting the rejection of atheists who clearly know no more about it than anybody else. (When it comes to mysticism, in fact, they know less.) But they don't really befriend the kind of mysticism I've been talking about. When all's said and done, the spiritual is an experience too good to throw away but impossible to explain. For many people some degree of spirituality is vital: their natures need it and as, we know, we get into terrible trouble when we go against the nature of things. You'd be a fool to disregard the dictates of your own nature because some people, with spiritual bits missing, disapprove.

13 Only One?

Physicists are allowed to think the most outlandish things and get away with it. What, Richard Feynman wondered, if there's just one electron in the cosmos instead of billions (and billions multiplied by billions)? What if that single electron appears in billions (and billions multiplied by billions) of places all at the same time. After all we know that individual particles can be in at least *two* places at once (don't we?). A strange-ish idea, but no more than that. Few baulk at it. Energy and matter are easily explained: they can arise spontaneously out of nothing. But what of consciousness? How can matter make it? Yet we take it for granted without a second thought (which we also take for granted).

14 Esoteric/Exoteric

Atheism is rampant these days, in spite of it's being as untenable as theism. Neither can be proved (or disproved). But there is another dimension which atheists miss: there are two levels of religion – exoteric and esoteric. In fact, you could say that religion is exoteric, while the esoteric is spiritual. Atheists attack the concrete, exoteric, literal kind of religion perhaps because they, too, are concrete-thinking literalists. Esoteric spirituality is also called mysticism, which can be defined as living for a moment in the presence of something Infinite – infinitely kind, infinitely still, unendingly unchanging.

Some of today's scientists (and philosophers) call themselves Brights, a term invented with shameless vulgarity by the American philosopher, Daniel C Dennett. Richard Dawkins is a Bright. Incompletes or Shallows might be more accurate. Out of Inge's two realms, they can live only in the material one. They also bring to mind Tennyson's poem about the swallow skimming the glittering surface of a lake catching gnats but ignorant of the deeps below.

15 Einstein's Other Theory

Einstein called himself a 'religious unbeliever'. In fact, he did believe – not in a personal God but, as I understand it, in 'a cosmic religious feeling' or 'a spirit manifest in the laws of the universe'. This belief, he said, was the best reason of all for doing science. Scientific research, in return, was the 'only creative religious activity of our time'. *Cosmic Religious Feeling* isn't often quoted in books about mysticism: perhaps it should be – as a new angle on mystic perception. It could go alongside Bucke's *Cosmic Consciousness*.

16 Unity for All

The idea of an underlying unity isn't peculiar to mysticism: it's now mainstream science: to physicists (and therefore most of the rest of us) that unity is energy. Some scientists go even farther. David Bohm, an American quantum physicist, thought reality might be like a ripple on a stream. The ripple is on the river but the river is also in the ripple, like a hologram. Explicate/Implicate, he called it. Thus you could say that the Explicate Eckhart is the ripple and the Godhead is the Implicate stream. The explicit man can see the entire river all at once because the whole is already implicit within him, as it is in everything. A nice idea though I'm not sure it gets us anywhere. Over-beliefs never do: the experience is all that matters: over-beliefs obscure it.

17 Misreading the Oracle

Back in the 1970s and '80s a few people in America were predicting a paradigm shift which would Easternise (or mysticise) and feminise the West. It had already begun with the fusion, as they saw it, of mysticism and quantum physics. I have to say I was taken up with these ideas myself and not only read as much as I could but also wrote one or two documentaries about them.

Books about the new physics and mysticism came out year by year. I began, I think, with Fritjof Capra's *The Tao of Physics* and over the next few years also bought his *The Turning Point* and *Uncommon Wisdom*. There was also Michael Talbot's *Mysticism and the New Physics* and Gary Zukav's *The Dancing Wu Li Masters* – among many others, too many to list.

The Paradigmists thought the West had reached a dead-end. Fritjof Capra, an Austrian physicist (and a prime mover of the idea), argued that the West was finished because its society, science and technology were all too mechanistic, masculine and Newtonian. It had to become mystical, feminine and Eastern. In his book, *The Turning Point*, there's a muted panic about the state of the world. Economists can't even understand inflation, he declared, so nothing can be done about it. (But it was understood: it was squeezed out in England. *Twice.*) He fretted about the arms race eight years before the fall of the Berlin Wall. The West was poisoning itself with chemicals and pollution. Diseases of old age and prosperity were killing people – cancer, strokes, heart attacks. Then, on the principle that if the whisky don't get you, the women must, the old who aren't ill go mad. Smog was about to change the climate (catalytic converters fixed that, I seem to remember, although lean-burn engines would have been better). Carbon dioxide didn't figure at all, which is strange given that within twenty years it was the evil of choice in the West. The other big, world-ending scares were acid rain, ozone holes, peak oil, the population explosion, desertification, deforestation.

Even odder was Capra's kow-towing to China, a closed society about which Westerners then knew little – not even that millions were being starved to death in Mao's Great Leaps Forward. We did know that it was, ironically, a Marxist dictatorship, a Western philosophy, not an Eastern one. Capra wrote a lot about *yin* and *yang*, the elemental forces which govern the cosmos. Looking back you have to ask: Why *yin* and *yang*? Greek philosophers had had similar ideas – Empedocles and *Love* and *Strife*, for example. If they are curiosities in the West, it's because they are of no practical use and explain very little. They're also no more mystical than gluons which may or may not stick quarks to each other.

The idea seems to have been that a quick, spiritual, evolution of Western Man (not Woman: she was spiritual already) was about to take place. We were all going to become mystics because physics, the leading science, had already passed its own turning point: now it was all about 'interconnectedness, relationship, dynamic patterns, and continual change and transformation.' This, the Paradigmists thought, was mystical although in fact it's the opposite: stillness is what the mystic meets: not the stillness of a decaying dynamic system – but stillness itself: not even the essence of stillness because it has no essence – just stillness. There was, in fact, a basic misunderstanding about the nature of mysticism. Nature may be holistic but mysticism is not about its day to day workings.

Also, even at its very lowest level, mysticism is a minority pursuit. What if the limiting factor, therefore, is neurophysiological – or, in other words, you need a physical aerial or antenna of some kind to tune in to passing mystic moments? No amount of amazement at the wonders of quantum physics could have brought on a spurt of biological evolution in such a short time. In any case, are mystics the fittest for survival in a hard-nosed world?

The supposed popularity of Schumacher's *small is beautiful* concept was another reason for thinking the West was changing. In fact, I wrote the script for a programme loosely based on Schumacher's book, *Small is Beautiful*. One item was about an Alternative Technology way of making hydroelectricity using nothing more than a crude propeller on a broomstick and a micro-chip to control the output. (Normally you need a finely engineered governor to control the inflow of water.) It was intended for Third World countries of which China was then one. Twenty years later China was building a coal-burning power station every week. When it comes to the choice between dinner and no-dinner, 'ego-action' beats 'ecoaction' every time. Even mystics eat.

And yet on the other hand, Paradigm shifters were right in sensing that parts, at least, of the West were changing. The only problem was the changes weren't spiritual but political. Partly it's been the feminisation or, more accurately, the infantilisation – the *yin*-ing – of the West. Political Correctness was perhaps not what the Paradigmists had in mind. They got the future wrong elsewhere, too – by failing to foresee, for example, the rise of China and Islam, about neither of which is there anything even remotely *yin*-ish at all.

I also remember being told off by a Marxist for reading Marilyn Ferguson's *The Aquarian Conspiracy* – a rhapsody to the paradigm shift which was then thought to be unstoppably underway. My rebuker's Marxist scorn for all things spiritual was scathing. She was a feminist but a far cry from Capra's vision of Woman as Embodied Spirituality. Mystical *yangs* stood no chance against political *yins* like her.

18 A Problem for Science

Otherwise, science has little to say about the spiritual. The mystic moment is brought on by a stoppage of thought. Getting that to happen while wired up or, worse, lying in a coffin-like brain scanner can't be easy. In the 1980s, Michael Persinger did it all in reverse by wiring up somebody's temporal lobes and firing magnetic impulses into them. 'An ethereal presence' was reported. We now know there's a 'God Slot' (or Spot?) in the brain. That might explain the Hirelings and Marthas – either they don't have one or it's stunted and shrivelled up.

The God Spot in the temporal lobes is also the place where epilepsy strikes. Some people once thought – perhaps still do – that mystical experiences and epileptic seizures are akin to each other. But, as Fraser Watts points out in *God For The 21st Century,* the epileptic episode is terrifying while the mystical one is the opposite. One can be life-spoiling, the other is always life-boosting.

Does the God-Spot/Slot prove that mysticism is all in the brain? Yes, of course. Who ever thought otherwise? Who *could* think otherwise? As long as we're made of star-created carbon we have no other way of interacting with the world.

19 Spirituality and Big John Wayne

How can a Western movie be spiritual? The clue is in the thinking of Thomas Carlyle, the Victorian historian, thinker, sage and mystic. We'll come back to him in a minute but meanwhile take as an example the 1976 film, *The Shootist,* starring John Wayne, Lauren Bacall and James Stewart. It's a simple story set in Carson City, Nevada, in January 1901. Queen Victoria's death fills the front page of the local paper: times are changing – the rawness of the old Frontier township is giving way to the future: next year an electrified tram will run through a city which already has running water and bathrooms: paving will follow soon.

Into this changing town rides J B Books (John Wayne), a fifty-seven year old gunmen. He's comes to see an old friend, Doc Hostetler (James Stewart), professionally. The diagnosis is cancer, the prognosis six to eight weeks to live, the last two or three in pain beyond the reach of the Doc's dollar bottle of laudanum.

The Doc suggests Books rents a room in a lodging house run by Bond Roger (Lauren Bacall) – a decent woman, he calls her – and her son Gillom (Ron Howard). This is, in fact, an elemental story of good versus evil. Bond soon begins to see the decency inherent in the self-confident, order-giving, dying gunman in her house. The Doc remarks that Books is one of the very few patients who volunteer to pay his fee, unasked. Books also spells out his simple code of honour to Gillom, after giving him a shooting lesson: essentially it's the Golden Rule – do unto others, expressed as leave me alone and I'll leave you alone.

Several men in the town stand for the opposite of decency, on a rising scale of badness from the mild greed of the undertaker (who'll go on to display Books's corpse, for a fee) and the barber (who'll sell the clippings of his hair). Higher up in the scale comes the pipsqueak journalist who's going to make his name by writing a lying biography of the dying shootist. Pure malice comes in the shape of the town Marshal.

Real evil, however, resides in three men. Cobb is a dairyman – a strange occupation for a bad lot, but he's mean and vicious, though cowardly. The second is the brother of a man Books shot dead some years ago. He has a spread out in the foothills and drives a new-fangled horseless carriage (so called by the boy, Gillom). The third man is the faro dealer in the big hotel. We see him shoot a man dead across the crowded bar room – over a distance of eighty-four feet and three inches, the malevolent Marshal gloatingly tells JB.

Rather than die in undignified pain, Books plans to go while he's still in control and can, at the same time, rid the world of a little of its evil. All the action takes place in a week. On the first (and last) Saturday, JB sends word to the three major villains that he'll be alone in the saloon of the Metropole Hotel at eleven o'clock on Monday morning. He even gets his best suit spruced up by the newly invented 'dry process cleaning'. He jokes about the smell of naphtha before saying good-bye to Bond and riding into town in the horse drawn tram, speaking kindly to a young girl fellow-passenger and giving the scarlet cushion – which until now he's used to ease his pain (and which he'd stolen from a whorehouse in Colorado) – to the old man who drives the contraption. It's a bright sunlit morning, a False Nevada Spring, and it's also his fifty-eighth birthday.

JB is a Victorian: The Metropole is the Edwardian 20th century. It has a vast saloon with alcoves for gamblers and is panelled opulently throughout with polished wood and mirrors. The three bad guys are waiting. JB orders a whisky and tosses a dollar bill onto the counter to pay for it. Cobb draws first in a panic and is easily shot down. The vengeful brother then picks up a table as a shield and is shot through it. All the same he wounds JB who falls behind the bar. The faro dealer creeps along below the counter only to be shot dead when he peers around the end. You think it's all over but why is JB still alive? That's not part of the plot, surely? Then the creepy bar-keep shoots him in the back with a double-barrelled shot gun.

Now young Gillom sidles into the saloon, picks up Books's fallen revolver and shoots the barman dead. And then throws the gun away. A small smile and nod of approval is JB's last action on earth.

And Carlyle? Where does he fit in? Like all mystics he had a sense of Greaterness which, by some quirk of character, he located in other people – in great men, heroes who are by definition strong. In *The Shootist* that is exactly the part John Wayne plays – a great man about to die who takes out some of the world's evil, leaving it a better place. The experience of any kind of greaterness, of course, is an undertone generator but Wayne also conveys a sense of sadness for the passing-away-ness of things (human life itself in this case) and stillness. These are the hallmarks of all true art which is, by definition, spiritual. There was also a strange grace about the man.

20 King Lear and Undertones

Great (and good) art expands consciousness and Shakespeare expands it more than anybody else. At the heart of his work is the insight that there's a divine order to things, to society in particular, and that disregarding or defying it always brings on disaster. This we see in *Lear* almost explicitly.

It's an unrelenting play but with one or two undertones. For example in the scene on the cliff. Lear wants to jump to his death but Edgar tricks him into thinking he's on the edge when he's still some way inland. He does this by lying about what he can see:

> Come on, sir; here's the place: stand still. How fearful
> And dizzy 'tis, to cast one's eyes so low!
> The crows and choughs that wing the midway air
> Show scarce so gross as beetles: half way down
> Hangs one that gathers samphire, dreadful trade!

Methinks he seems no bigger than his head:
The fishermen, that walk upon the beach,
Appear like mice; and yond tall anchoring bark,
Diminish'd to her cock; her cock, a buoy
Almost too small for sight: the murmuring surge,
That on the unnumber'd idle pebbles chafes,
Cannot be heard so high. I'll look no more;
Lest my brain turn, and the deficient sight
Topple down headlong.

What are the undertones? The samphire, its gatherers, the 'anchoring bark', the idle pebbles on the soundless beach and the soundless sea itself.

21 Strato the Presumptuous

Strato was the man who, in the 3rd century BC, took over the Lyceum on Aristotle's death. He left us the Stratonician Presumption: the presumption is that there is no God and if you want to believe in one it's up to you to prove that He exists. Nobody ever has. Christianity is also inherently ridiculous to the literal Post-Enlightenment mind, what with virgin births and the dead rising from the grave or a man walking on the sea. For some people there's also something distasteful about all that blood and blighted fig trees.

Can we get around Strato? At one time Cardinal Newman worried about the problem of Probabilities. Could it destroy Certainty? Keble said look at it from the opposite point of view: belief in God gives meaning to what is otherwise meaningless: it increases and completes us in every way. The probability must therefore be that there's something essential and inbuilt about the need for it.

Newman picked up another idea from St Clement (or Origen). We know for a fact (or as certainly as we can know anything) that our senses are limited – why then do we assume they tell us the truth, the whole truth and nothing but the truth? Some people seem to have a sixth sense about a spiritual dimension. Given that the senses are at best a bit blunt, who can say they're wrong?

Instinctively, however, we're all materialists now and that's a hard mindset from which to break free. Yet what could be harder to accept than the extraordinary fact of consciousness and thought? They're so much odder than matter which is itself so extraordinary as to be barely believable. Some scientists argue that the laws governing the universe are so suspiciously unlikely that they could well have been set in place specifically to force consciousness to evolve.

Agnosticism is the only honest *opinion,* I suppose. But the experience of something greater than the self is not an opinion: it's a fact. What we can't know, intellectually and with certainty, is what it all means, exactly.

22   Art and the NT

Christianity is flexible and open to evolution and, as Origen said, spiritual truths don't have to be literally true. Given that, is it possible to accept Christianity? What is its esoteric, non-literal heart? One of its mystical insights is that death is impossible because something in you is eternal. For the exoteric mind, this is graphically demonstrate by The Resurrection, which you don't have to take literally.

If art is spiritual, the New Testament has it – it's a narrative, a story. If poetry is spiritual, the Tyndale/King James's Bible is full of it. 'Come to me all ye who labour and are heavy laden and I will give you rest.' 'In my Father's house are many mansions.' 'My peace I give unto you.' It's also an instruction manual on how to reach spiritual maturity: get rid of ego, do unto others, love thy neighbour, don't cling to things (clinging to riches is the problem, not the riches themselves).

23   Paracletism and the Goldilocks Zone

Christianity isn't always to the taste of the introverted. Narrative rarely appeals to them – the mystic moment is a point: it's not a line, it's an out of the blue suddenness. To this kind of temperament, God the Father is a bit too remote, while God the Son is too close and too human for introverts who are uncomfortable with people, even divine ones. Some extreme introverts recoil from doing anything in public: sinking into a crowd in a theatre and being controlled by actors on the stage is distasteful to them. Being part of a congregation is a bit too much like being part of a pack – flock is apt. There's a brutality about crowds and congregations which repels.

But the Trinity comes up trumps for introverts with the Paraclete or Holy Ghost (Spirit, these days). The Paraclete is abroad in the world, finely nebulous and unconcrete, and accessible. Holy Remoteness is too cold and far away, Sonship is too nearby and hot: Paracletism is the introvert's Goldilocks Zone.

24 A Faith That Failed

The Neoplatonism of Plotinus is the one mystic system which comes closest to science. It could well have become the West's religion. That it didn't is probably because it's too esoteric: there's nothing there for Hirelings or Marthas to get their hands on. But to Inge, Plotinus was the greatest of the mystic-philosophers. More than that, his was the deepest spiritual philosophy possible to mankind and it came at the end of one and half thousand years of uninterrupted thought starting with the Pre-Socratics of Ionia. Neoplatonism sustained Inge for most of his life. Plotinus taught three things: reality is spiritual: you can know it: the cosmos is good, sacred, and a single entity and unity.

At the centre is the Logos or the nature of things or the rules governing us all. We can call it Consciousness. Out of it comes waves of lesser consciousness which solidify as matter, including us, although in our souls we also stay partly immaterial. To science, the underlying energy of the universe did, and does, solidify into matter, embedded in which is immaterial consciousness.

25   Problems for Monotheists

The question of evil in a world made by Goodness has bothered monotheists for centuries. Similar ideas to explain it keep cropping up. Dionysius the Areopagite thought evil was good in the wrong place, just as dirt is. In the *Purgatorio,* Virgil told Dante that sin is love taken to extremes: love of food is good but taken too far it becomes the sin of gluttony. This doesn't contradict the Neoplatonist idea that sin is disobeying the laws of nature – you know gluttony is wrong because the results are bad. A more modern, Ruskinian, explanation is that sin is what diminishes and decreases you, diverting you from the route decreed by your nature. Again this doesn't contradict Dante. The Seven Deadly Sins diminish you, also, by defying the the nature of things.

Walter Hilton, author of the 14th century *Ladder of Perfection,* said sin is lack of light and love. 'It is false inordinate love of thyself, from whence flow all the deadly things'. In other words, it's a distortion of the way things should be. This basic idea is common, without exception, to mysticism. *The German Theology* said: 'The more self and me, the more of sin, and wickedness.' 'Be simply and wholly bereft of self.' 'As long as a man seek his own highest good .... he will never find it.' *The German Theology* also said sin is separation from God through ego. You're saved, therefore, by rising above it. Tauler said: 'we must lop and prune vices, not nature, which is itself good and noble'.

And what of Hell? How can a loving God condemn people who never asked to be born in the first place? Calvinism is worse: it believes (believed?) that the soul's creator knew which soul was to suffer eternal torment before it was created. There's a kind of madness in all of this.

Not unnaturally, given their vision, even mystics who are also monotheists doubt the fires of hell. Boehme, for example, said there's nothing supernatural about Redemption – it's a righting of wrongs. If you're damned, you've damned yourself and only you can you get yourself out of it by putting right the bad things you've done. In 'the time of the lilies' all nature will be set free from bondage.

None of this, of course, is a problem for mystics of the Neoplatonist or Eckhartian school since, for them, the soul's apex and the Ultimate are the same thing and so there is no eternal Hell. Eckhart said Heaven and Hell are states of mind, not places: Hell is separation from God. Tauler said separation from God is the source of all misery and is the pain of Hell. Ego is the separator. Ego is also Original Sin, a deviation.

26 Continuum

Many people ask why, if God is good, do we have death, bad weather and earthquakes? Religious scientists, such as John Polkinghorne – who is both a quantum physicist and an ordained priest – have another take on it. People who ask for a pain-free universe are calling for a continuum. But a continuum is so smooth, so unbroken, so without energy, hotspots, hills and valleys that it's a kind of nothingness. The lesson is that, without pain, we'd live in a blandness which, in effect, is death. Love and loving-kindness would be unknowable, undetectable, impossible. In short, you might be alive but you wouldn't know it.

In turn, that raises a new question: how can mystics at the extreme end of the scale detect the Ultimate if it's changeless and unmoving? Is, in other words, a continuum? Nobody has any idea. As always we come back to the fact that we're dealing with an experience which is out of reach of the intellect.

27 Flower Power Failure

Speaking in 1899, Dean Inge speculated that the future would have to learn things which his own generation would have been unable to bear. Well, his future is now our past and we know for a fact that the 20th century experienced catastrophes which even the 20th century was barely able to face. Fifty years after his 1899 lectures, Inge knew these things for himself – he'd lived through the two World Wars and written his last book only four or five years after the 12th Armoured Brigade had surrounded Belsen.

And yet, in spite of everything and against all the odds, he still thought the way forward for the West was through spiritual religion – a mix of New Testament Christianity and the esotericism of Neoplatonism. When that happened, religion would have something for everybody, from the professor to his kitchen-maid (people got away with saying that kind of thing back then).

He wasn't the only one whose predictions were hopelessly wrong. Spiritual people tend to be baffled, I suspect, by the unspirituality of others. In the 1960s, Sir Alister Hardy, a biologist by profession and a mystic by birth, had hoped for a religious revival based on what he called 'experimental faith': treat faith as a hypothesis and then test it by practice. If your life isn't improved, I suppose you'd say the hypothesis had been falsified or proved wrong. He was an old man at the time of the Zen and Flower Power crazes in the hippie colonies on the West Coast and perhaps was taken in. That, or wishful thinking.

28 A Lack of Churchly Glue?

Inge wrote: 'We live in two worlds which are so far related to each other that if we deny all reality to either of them, the other fades away.' Today the spiritual world for many – most – has faded. Some might blame science but Darwinism, for example, was fairly easily accepted and doesn't clash. Geology was a bigger problem because it falsified *Genesis,* but then again not fatally: myths can be spiritually true even if factually or literally wrong. No, the decline of the spiritual is, overwhelmingly, a result of the Enlightenment and its core philosophy of doubt. But has Protestantism also something to do with it, in a minor degree?

Inge said mysticism is a churchly glue which Protestant churches can't get enough of. There have been a quite a few Protestant mystics – Boehme, Fox, the Cambridge Platonists, Wesley, Law, Jonathan Edwards among (many) others. In the 17th century 'seekers' and 'waiters' sought (or waited) for a heavenly guidance which rarely came. The Philadelphians, who smacked of visionary quackery, didn't outlive the death of their leader, Mrs Jane Leade. All the same, it does seem a bit surprising that Protestantism isn't chockfull of mystics given that they deny any need for intermediaries. Luther was contemptuous of mystics and relied solely on the Bible. (The 17th century German mystic poet, Angelus Silesius, converted to Catholicism to get away from the unwelcoming Lutheran church into which he'd been born.) The reason, I suppose, is an over-reliance on written and spoken words. Mysticism comes when the intellect goes. A system which encourages one, discourages the other. The anomaly is the 19th century when so many writers and artists were quietly mystical.

29 Mrs Flaxman and the Spiritual

The physical shape of most human beings is far from divine. Few physiques can evoke mystic moments unless, like Blake, you can see divinity in them, which must be unlikely at the best of times.

Then I came across a portrait of Mrs Flaxman, wife of the sculptor (who was also Blake's friend). It was painted in 1797 and, although I don't know Mrs Flaxman's age at the time, her husband was forty-four so presumably she was around forty or a bit younger herself.

Her painter, Henry Howard, is not well known and not well thought of when he is. But in this one painting, he captured that core of stillness and sadness which is essential to mystic insight. It's an astonishing *tour de force*.

30 Icons

Some icons are astonishing in their impact. For most, however, the undertones are more in the idea than in the image – or at least, perhaps, it is for people not brought up with them. They are of course an Orthodox art form and so, unsurprisingly, the concept behind them is Plato's *Idea* (or image) or *Form* – his intellectualising of his mystic vision of unchanging perfection. Some say icons are like doors opening on to paradise. They're also said to be a form of prayer – but then Father Hopkins thought all art is, or should be.

Heaven touches earth in an icon. If what is painted is heaven, then what it's painted on (and with) is Earth: the wooden panel is vegetable: the brushes made of hog bristles are animal: the gold and gesso are mineral. An icon is in harmony with God and also reveals God's harmony. Translucence, a common technique, is the luminosity of the Holy Spirit. Gold leaf is God's light and therefore casts no shadows. Halo'd figures have been deified – not made into God but made God-like.

Iconography, it seems, can be divided into three periods: pre- and post-Iconoclasm, and then, thirdly, the last few years of the 20th century. The Iconoclasm began in 726 and lasted for a century or so. The Byzantine Emperor Leo III, who was originally behind the ban (and burnings), thought icons could be used as graven images. Some people could, I suppose, worship them exoterically but, used esoterically, they are really no more than thought-stopping devices.

Some say icons evolved from Egyptian funerary pictures in the late Roman Empire. Only a few paintings from Late Antiquity survived the great Iconoclasm but the ones that did are a revelation – they're much more modern looking than later ones. Those from St Catherine's Monastery, in Sinai, dating from the 6th Century, seem to be the main survivors. Such, for example, as *St Peter* with his carefully combed and parted hair and beard of a colour hard to put a name to – green-blue? blue-green? If luminosity is the Holy Spirit then here the Paraclete is shining through. There's a calmness and a sadness in the eyes as well as that eternal gaze looking out at us from across the bar of Heaven.

The Blessing Christ from the same time and place could well be the most astonishing icon of them all with its compelling and very modern face. One hand holds up a book, presumably *The Bible*, the other is held up in blessing. Background and halo hardly matter because you don't really see them. The whole focus is on the figure's eyes. Are they accusing, imploring, hurt by betrayal, let down? The Divine is also revealed through stillness. Sadness is there too, not so much sadness for things as for fallen humanity itself.

112

Post-Iconoclasm, icons became more stylised: eyes, for example, became bigger, noses and mouths smaller: the eye is a spiritual window. The Serbian *Archangel Michael* from the 14th century is a good example of the later more stylised icons. He's a bit off-putting, I think, with a cruel mouth and eyes squinting with dislike of whatever they see – i.e. *you*. He carries an orb and sceptre to show his authority over the world – not a comforting thought given his hard and hostile face.

Some modern icons certainly work better. Take, for example, the icon of *St George* in the Orthodox monastery of St Anthony and St Cuthbert in Shropshire. It even works as allegory – the warrior-saint slays the inner dragons of ego and sin. The stare is there but it's no longer hostile. The eyes draw you into the picture which is, of course, the Other Side. All the same, however, it lacks that extraordinary power – in fact it's a bit soppy – of the unknown iconographer who painted *The Blessing Christ* somewhere between 500 and 600. We've retrogressed in that regard.

31 Paul Sandby RA at the RA

Paul Sandby (1731-1809) is usually and rather cumbersomely called the 'father of modern landscape painting in watercolours'. He's also the man who invented the aquatint (the *aqua* is *aquafortis* – acid: acid, not metal tools, cuts away copper to make a softer, more watercolour-like print). On top of all that he opened up a market for pictures and prints of the landscapes, antiquities and people of his own country. An important man, then, in the history of things and the Royal Academy held an exhibition of his paintings and etchings in the summer of 2010. A lot of his work was made expressly to be printed in books: it shows – only two pictures were better viewed hung on a wall. For the others, you were better off sitting under the murals in the café and looking at the catalogue.

The 1776 aquatint, *The Iron Forge between Dolgelli and* *Barmouth in Merionethshire*, is one of the two which were best looked at on the wall, even if you had to crane your neck a bit.

There's smoke from the forge, a rush of water from the leat, water pouring over a small fall, a crag white and ghost-like on the hills behind. A cowherd drives cattle. Trees lean over a cliff in the foreground to the left. It's good but doesn't compare in power to Samuel Palmer's Welsh paintings seventy years later. Palmer, of course, was a mystic.

Caernarvon Castle by Moonlight also works well on the wall in a mildly mind-arresting way. A fire on the terrace lights up a row of four windows, like moonlight. A blaze behind the castle to the right shines on what might be a boat building yard. A meteor streaks through the sky. Moonlight lies on the sea in the Menai Straits. One side of the tower is moonlit, the rest is in shadow. Figures on the shore lead (haul?) a reluctant horse by its bridle. It's not realistic – moonlight is never that bright. But lightness in darkness does symbolise the mystic state.

Mystically speaking, *The Devil's Cave, Castleton, Derbyshire* (August 1774) is one of the best. Small huts and tiny figures line the path below great white crags. Clumps of trees grow high on ledges in the rock. These crags are sunlit: the ones on the left of the picture are in the shade. Then there's the great gaping mouth of the cave – a cavern, in fact – with views into its throat. A two storey house just in front of the cave is reduced to hut-size by the scale of it all. Pale yellow is the dominant colour, except for a blue stream flowing in front of the onlooker at the bottom of the page. The whole is very delicately done in pen, ink and watercolour over graphite.

Above the painting there is, in fine calligraphy, a long caption. In it Sandby calls the cave 'stupendous'. Poor people, it turns out, lived in the huts along the path leading to the cavern. Essentially they were beggars living off hand-outs from visitors. Knowing that doesn't help the picture's undertones: emotions, such as pity, get in the way.

Paul Sandby's brother, Thomas, was a lifelong collaborator. If Paul was no mystic, Thomas seems to have been a-mystical – there is, for example, a terrible emptiness about his picture of *Nottingham Market Square* (1740s). This Nottingham (where the brothers were born) is a handsome place, civilised, elegant and proportioned. The Malt Cross is a dome held on slender pillars. Seven trees in a row are encircled by benches. An elegant colonnade curves gracefully. There are only two figures, vaguely sketched and very small. But the emptiness is not because of the absence of people: this is about an emptiness at the heart of things for which there is no comfort, although for the lesser mystic it can possibly generate desolation undertones.

That said, there's a beautiful clarity about the work of both brothers, except for Paul's ugly and malicious caricatures of Hogarth. Paul's prints of street traders, for example, are not just historically interesting, they have a power in their own right: milkmaids, hucksters, vendors of fish, tripe and hosiery. They're arresting though you can see also the sadness in their faces – or was that added by Sandby?

So is Sandby a catalyst for mystics? More, I'd say, a provider of undertones, the lowest level of mysticism. Undertones can be all the more powerful because, though they arrive in small doses, they're frequent and in the end they all add up to something bigger.

You can pick out something of the way this is done in Sandby's *The Old Welsh Bridge at Shrewsbury*, 1772. To begin with, there's a certain imprecision and mysteriousness about it, half revealed by failing light, half hidden by falling night. The arches lead to a different kind of light and to something even more evocative – the last of the day's light faint on the old stone of a tower. You look through the arches at Severn barges moored to the bank of the river. Rivers matter, mystically speaking.

Somehow also Sandby has stopped time. It's 1772 and the dimly seen figures are in the dress of the day. Yet time here has ended, made to disappear. Except in some strange way time-past is still time-present, as Eliot put it. This is unchangingness in change. Look at the tower and you see what Housman saw in his poem, *The Welsh Marches*:

The vanquished eve, as night prevails,
Bleeds upon the road to Wales.

Is it because of the dark colours, the choice of colours, the vagueness, the half-seen-ness of it all which makes it work? It works until you try to take it apart. Undertones, and all higher layers of mysticism, come only when thinking stops.

32 Kandinsky

Kandinsky, the Russian painter, was one of the dozens of artists and writers who made the 19th century such a mystic hotspot. He thought a work of art is a new world, a cosmic event. Abstract art is beyond time, space and the material world and expresses a deeper reality. Art is a mystery which explores Mystery. Today we demystify everything – art is to explore our material selves, preferably with a sexual or political slant. We've evacuated one of Inge's two worlds, abandoned that underlying unity, and who can claim we're the better for it?

33 Sargent and the Sea: Immaturity and Promise

In the summer of 2010 the Royal Academy held an exhibition of the early paintings of John Singer Sargent. Very early paintings, in fact: when he painted them he was still only a youth or a very young man between eighteen and twenty-three (1874-79). Some critics panned the art on display there, and not without reason. For part of this time he was still a student at an *atelier* in Paris. Many of the paintings and sketches were apprentice work, little more than juvenilia. His Mediterranean harbours, for instance, just don't work. *Whitby Fishing Boats* is later – 1884, when Sargent was twenty-eight – and it doesn't work either: the sea looks like an oil spill. In another picture, set on a Moroccan beach, fishing nets spread out to dry look like tar or thick oil from a wrecked tanker off-shore. *Seascape with Rocks* (c 1875-77) brings to mind the end of the world in H G Wells's *The Time Machine*. The rocks are like softened beetroot, the sea like oil-thickened juice.

Sargent's early life was unusual. He was born in Florence to American parents who spent their time criss-crossing Europe. His father was a doctor but his family had been ship owners in America since the 17th century. John Singer (his mother's maiden name) Sargent grew up in Europe speaking four languages. In 1876, when he was nineteen, his mother took him and his sister to America for the first time (the age of majority then was twenty-one, so in law he was still a minor). They stayed only four months before re-crossing the Atlantic. These voyages gave him material for his never-repeated blue water paintings. Nobody before him, it seems, had taken the open sea as a subject in itself without reference either to people or the shore. In this he was an originator.

Having said all that, there is more than mere promise in several of these very early works: there are stirrings of mystic moments and, in one portrait, the full-blown thing. Later, he made his fortune, of course, painting fashionable people and gave up on the sea. A pity because he had a gift for seascapes.

For a start, I think you can detect desolation experiences in some of his sea paintings. *The Derelict* c1876 (oil on canvas) is really only a closer view of *Atlantic Sunset* also c 1876 (also oil on canvas). The same derelict ship is in both. At first glance it looks like a stranded wreck. But, we learn from the catalogue, ships which became unseaworthy through fire or storm were often abandoned in mid-ocean in the Victorian period. At any given time in the North Atlantic shipping lanes there were around twenty – nearly a thousand all told between 1887-1891.

In both paintings we're standing on the deck of a passenger liner in the chill of an Atlantic sunset. The vast, frightening sea stretches to the end of the world in muted menace. The comfort of the heat of the sun is gone. The gold coloured sea is utterly alien. There, on the beam, is stillness and sadness in the shape of a dying ship. At one time people spoke of ships and boats as 'she', as though they were alive. And there is this human-created 'she' dying in this alien yellow water. Soon she'll sink to the even more alien bottom of the sea. Her main and fore masts half gone and her mizzen is down to a stump. No bowsprit points at the strange sky. A bank of blue cloud lines the horizon, picture-wide, with orange-grey and white streaks above.

Of the two, *The Derelict* is the stronger. The sea is not so calm and there are distant troughs in the waves. Everything, the ship included, is in sharper focus.

Both these pictures were re-discovered – or even discovered – only recently, along with *Seascape* (also c 1876, also oil on canvas). Here the horizon is more distant and more distinctly a line of sea and not a cloud bank. A great gap in the clouds lets through pale yellow sunlight which falls on the sea close to the horizon, but also shimmers on the spectator's side of the picture behind a line of waves with spindrift whipping from their crests. You'd need at least a Force Six on the Beaufort Scale to raise a sea like that and, since the rest of the water is calm, we assume this ridge of water is the ship's wake. We are, then, standing at ship's rail.

En Route pour la Pêche, 1877-78, (oil on canvas) is both immature and striking. It's an arresting, impressionist-like painting of a group of women and two children on their way to the oyster beds which are seen as bright blue oblongs to the left. They walk across sand with a lighthouse in the background. Distant figures, just quick brush strokes, are already wading through low tide to the beds. Fishing smacks, two with sails half hoisted, lie berthed on the far beach. The sky is blue and white with brush-clouds.

To begin with, there seems to be nothing mystic about it. It's curiously static yet without stillness. For a start, the women aren't walking. Each clogged foot is set on the sand, not apart as in a stride: the feet are as close together as a statues on a narrow plinth. When you look closer, though, you notice something special about the leading figure, a young woman. She wears a blue blouse, a grey mid-calf skirt, grey clogs, and a white head scarf. The top and nape of the scarf is lit by pale sunlight. She holds an oyster basket on her hip with both hands: on her left wrist, sunlit and only sketched in, she wears a bangle of sorts. The interest is in her face. We see it only from the side, she's looking away. In it, though, there's the stillness and the sadness that makes a work great and not just workaday, however well done. The face is beautiful, mysterious, arresting, sad and still. Sargent's later genius for portraits is already on show. It was wired-in, untaught. Whatever the critics said, the whole thing was worthwhile for that face alone.

34 An 'Absence of Mind'

At least three books with similar themes – the decline of the West – came out in 2010. In *Absence of Mind*, the novelist Marilynne Robinson argues that the West has crossed a threshold into a new age, different almost in kind from what's gone before, certainly very different in degree. What has been lost is inwardness, access to the inner world where the spiritual seems to arise. The past is discounted, disconnected, dismissed and scorned. Thought itself has been fractured. The cause is a stunted scientific mindset which Marilynne Robinson calls parascience, the beginnings of which she dates back to Auguste Comte in the 1840s.

All the other Schools behind parascience are also old – Nietzsche, Freud, Darwin, (Marx?), as well as newer ones such as sociology. (All, apart from Darwinism, are surely discredited?) None of their ideas connect one with another. All are disparate and contradictory except for one common meeting point: all believe that ordinary people don't know who they are, what they are, or why they are.

Parascience arrogantly explains us to ourselves through a series of generalisations, often based on cherry-picked data. What all of them also do is evade or avoid the inner world of the mind. Religion is misunderstood even though Comte, the founding member, proposed a new religion to replace the old – Humanity, the Grand Being. But that's forgotten, too. Dennett sees religion, erroneously, as a social system. William James saw it, accurately, as a personal experience. Dennett sees only the exoteric, whereas James homes in unerringly on the esoteric.

35 A Spiritual Swamp?

Speaking in 1899, Inge said: 'when the free current of the religious life is dammed up ... it turns into a swamp, and poisons human society'. Over a hundred years later, in England at least, the current is well and truly dammed up. Inge went on: 'The constructive task which lies before the (20th century) is to spiritualise science, as morality and art have already been spiritualised.' Today, though, art and morality have been de-spiritualised and science itself has been corrupted.

The history of Quakerism is a good way to trace the decay of the spiritual in the West. Fox, the founding Quaker, called the mystic moment a meeting with the Inward Light. Submitting to it leads you to what is right. It's 'before Time and in Time'. 'Mind the Light and dwell with it and it will keep you atop of all the world.' Fox sometimes called it the Topstone. All have it to some degree, he thought, though some more than others, and we should to be faithful to it up our limits. By obeying it we prime ourselves for a meeting with the Divine. How things have changed. Inner Lights for many Quakers nowadays are the standard second-hand ideas of the left-wing political mindset.

36   The Pre-Tar Water Bishop Berkeley

The Bishop's philosophical work was all done long before he was a bishop and not long after he'd reached his majority: all was finished in fact by the age of twenty-five. He was a young man opposing the materialism of an old one (as he saw John Locke). Locke's mechanical, clockwork, machine-tooled cosmos appalled him and he picked out what he thought were its contradictions. Matter (Locke said – and as I understand it) creates ideas in the mind which the mind then uses to create images of matter. But how, Berkeley questioned, can you even know that matter exists outside the mind when you can only sample it from within? And, if matter does exist, how can you be sure that the image in your mind is even remotely like the reality outside it? How do you know it isn't twisted out of shape?

More than that, Berkeley worried that materialism would undermine theism and the morals which he supposed depend on it. After all, if mind and soul are merely aspects of matter, we could well be mortal and what's to stop depravity then? His problem was not mystical at all but a prosaically Age of Reason one.

Berkeley's solution? There's no such thing as matter. Matter doesn't exist outside a mind. Matter doesn't create ideas: ideas create matter. Matter therefore disappears when a mind isn't paying attention to it. And the cause of these ideas of matter? God. That's why matter is never not there: God's attention never strays or wanders.

Ronald Knox wrote a limerick about it:

There was a young man who said 'God
Must find it exceedingly odd
To think that the tree
Should continue to be
When there's no one about in the quad.'

'Dear Sir: Your astonishment's odd;
I am always about in the quad.
And that's why the tree
Will continue to be
Since observed by, Yours faithfully, God.'

Idealism is a nice idea, ridiculous to us only because we're such hardened materialists. Nor is idealism really very peculiar. You *do* have images of matter in your immaterial mind. Why, then, can't consciousness be primary? Nobody knows.

37 Wittgenstein: a Closet Mystic?

The odd thing about Wittgenstein is that he's said to have had a mystical experience while serving with the Austrian army on the Eastern Front in the Great War. The trigger was Tolstoy. At the same time he was carrying in his kitbag the manuscript of his *Tractatus Logico-Philosophicus* in which he argued that metaphysics is out of bounds because we can't think about it because we don't have the words to do so, and we can't speak about it because we can't think about it. 'Whereof one cannot speak, thereof one must remain silent.' He then gave up on philosophy because, as far as I can make out, he'd caught himself cheating – using complicated abstract arguments in a world composed only of simple facts.

What he meant by 'facts' nobody seems to know. However, a mystical experience *is* a fact, whatever else it isn't. Twenty odd years later, in the *Blue* and *Brown Books,* he said: 'The limits of my language are the limits of my reality.' But the mystical experience, of which we can't speak, is a reality also.

You can understand somebody like Hume dismissing the mystical, because the limits of his understanding were pretty narrow, but not a man who'd had his own mystic moment.

38 The Flaws in Flew's Deism

Antony Flew, the philosopher, died in April (2010). He was eighty-seven. For sixty-six of those years (1938-2004) he was an atheist. Then, aged eighty-one, he converted to a kind of deism, though his deity was even more remote than the Age of Reason clock-maker. His new positive belief, like his old negative one, came about through reason although what convinced him is, in fact, only the Aquinan Argument from Design up-dated by DNA's double helix which he thought was just too complex to have evolved by itself unaided.

Flew's obituary in *The Daily Telegraph* generated a few letters. The first was from a lady in California, a fellow atheist, who said Flew wasn't quite right in the head at the time of his conversion. The Rev. Peter Mullen, a City of London vicar, wrote to say that Flew was a theist and no deist: he'd been influenced by the 'moral and spiritual power of the Gospels, as well as by Tom Wright's arguments supporting the Resurrection.

Professor Haldane of St Andrew's University thought that although Flew had been in decline he'd still been sharp enough to think of himself as an 'Einsteinian deist' and that the proof for this belief was in the intelligence you can see at work in the cosmos. Evolutionary theory doesn't disprove the argument from design.

Next, and more perceptively, a C J G Macey said he'd been 'responsible' for publishing Flew's 1976 *The Presumption of Atheism*. 'I believe that Flew, perhaps despite himself, underwent, not a change of mind, but a change of heart.' That sounds more likely: why else spend a lifetime fiddling with something you think is wrong and can't believe in? Because, perhaps, in your heart you wanted to believe in it all along?

Relying on reason is the flaw in all this. The experience comes when reason is aborted. Even 'undertones' – those amorphous spiritual meanings surrounding things – have nothing to do with intellect or thought. Think about them and they lose their (non-rational) meaning.

39 Minor Third

Of all the arts, music was the one most commonly quoted as an ecstasy-trigger in answer to Marghanita Laski's questionnaire about mysticism. People in those far-off days (sixty years and more ago and counting) thought some things were intrinsically better than others. High art was better than low. So Laski wondered if high brow music were a bigger trigger of mystic moments than the low brow.

Not necessarily. Whatever stills the mind works. Some folk music can do this, some pop songs too. Not all classical music can (the bulk of it in fact can't). Melodies of the kind once called haunting seem to be vital, and a central quietness along with a sense of sadness for the loneliness of things. Few musical scores will usher in full mind-blown mystical union, but many more can release undertones. Nor does the voice have to be trained, or even good. A raucous croak like Rod Stewart singing *Sailing* gets close to the real thing.

One chapter in *Undertones: Mild Mysticism in an Age of Umber* is about the music of Vaughan Williams (chosen because he was a mystic in his own right). His *Fantasia on Greensleeves*, the book concludes, generates mystic moments and undertones through its inherent repose and sadness. This, apparently, is because it's in the Minor Third, the classic way of expressing sadness in music. Research (in 2010) at Tufts University in Massachusetts possibly shows that the same sadness-inducing rules of the Minor Third apply to speech as well.

The spoken Minor Third is presumably the Dying Fall of poetry, and T S Eliot's *The Love Song of J Alfred Prufrock* in particular:

For I have known them all already, known them all –
Have known the evenings, mornings, afternoons,
I have measured out my life with coffee spoons;
I know the voices dying with a dying fall
Beneath the music from a farther room.
So how should I presume?

Darwin suggested that, before there was speech, there was a kind of mouth music through which moods, and possibly simple ideas, were put over in a kind of sing-song-withoutwords. Gibbons do so to this day. Human – or hominid? – singer-speakers would have expressed feelings of sadness, presumably, through the three semi-tones of the Minor Third and this was carried over into pure speech when language and music went their separate ways. Which is all very well, but why are these three semi-tones sad and therefore also mystical?

40 Arias

Some time in the summer of 2010, BBC, Radio 3 ran a survey to find 'the nation's favourite aria'. It turned out to be Purcell's lament 'When I am laid in earth' from *Dido and Aeneas*. All the other nine top arias, as it happened, were just as sad. One critic thought it was all to do with bad news – the economy, the oil leak in the Gulf of Mexico, the World Cup (what happened there?). It's a sign of the times that a concrete cause is always looked for.

As we've seen, sadness and repose are the chief ingredients of the spiritual in art. But why, in a secular age, do they appeal to so many people?

41 Rebuked

In *Undertones: Mild Mysticism in an Age of Umber* I claimed (asserted?) that only three pieces of music by Vaughan Williams were likely to induce low-level ecstatic experiences. I was wrong, or at least spoke only for myself. One lady who answered Laski's questionnaire was mystically moved by VW's 'penultimate' symphony. All told, she'd been moved nearly twenty times by very nearly twenty triggers: love, Mozart, Beethoven's 9th, VW's 5th, '*King Lear*' (even Laski put this in inverted commas – a whole two-hour state of ecstasy?), landscape, storm at sea, flying, writing, singing (German lieder, Irish folk songs), Italian opera.

Inspiration, the lady said, had the same starting point as ecstasy except that ecstasy enlarged you while inspiration diminished. What did she mean by that, I wonder? That the hard work which follows inspiration left her drained? Inspiration, she did add, was like giving birth. Who she was we don't know, nor what she did, how old she was or where she lived or who her husband was (she had children and so, in the 1950s, probably had one). It'd be nice to know more.

42 Taiko

It's extraordinary how stretched skin beaten with sticks can be so otherworldly. Banging a drum rhythmically isn't in the least mystical, unless it beats the mind into unconsciousness (which is why Shamans in Siberia played drums). Taiko drumming is altogether higher. It's been around for only thirty or forty years but Zen, I suspect, is in there somewhere and, additionally, priests have been playing drums in Shinto temples for two and half millennia.

The greatest – the most dramatic – drum is perhaps as big as a hogshead, smaller ones are like firkins, kilderkins or kegs. Others match side, snare or kettle drums. Between them they make patterns of sound, like poetry but without the rigidity. Some pieces tell a story – one is of fishermen hauling nets. It's also very visual. Beating the skin of a taiko drum has all the ceremony and courtesy of sumo wrestling. Bodies are braced and bent backward, arms swung wide in great revolving circles. Some times the arms seem to flail bonelessly, only the sticks being rigid. The whole performance is perfectly synchronised and choreographed – the stage is never still, except when, almost in the lotus position, the drummers sit bolt up-right, wrists pivoting.

Small brass cymbals are polished till they glitter. They're called *chappa*. The high spot is when the players toss a sound from one to the other, faster and faster, until the sound is pitched high in the air. The players look up to see where it is. One of them catches it before it hits the ground.

Often there's an underlying sadness, which raises the music to a higher plane, particularly when the flute plays a plaintive tune. (The bamboo flute sound is inherently sad, in a spiritual way, in any case.) There's a coarseness about Western drumming (other than the military which is there to mark the time in marches) and crudeness kills the mystic. This drumming isn't and doesn't. It opens the window.

43 Blake on the Gothic

Ruskin and Pugin were the joint originators of the Gothic Revival. Yet Blake, long before either of them, had similar ideas. Writing (about Virgil) in 1820 he said that the Grecian is calculated and mathematical whereas Gothic is living and alive. Calculation is of this earth, while whatever lives is eternal (and holy). According to Kathleen Raine, Blake saw St Paul's Cathedral as 'a monument of Deism, the 'natural religion' of the Enlightenment, of Newton's 'Pantocrator', demiurge of the mechanistic universe, of science.' Reason in the shape of Bacon, Newton, Locke, and of science and empiricism was, for him, the enemy of life, blinding our inborn mystical sight.

Blake, a time-served engraver, had been such an awkward apprentice that his master had set him to work, all on his own, copying the carvings in Westminster Abbey. Gothic sculpture, Blake concluded, was not about capturing a likeness in stone – it exposed the essence of a thing: not a king but kingship, not a knight but courage, not a lady but grace itself. The sinuosity of the lines in all his own drawings derive from the Gothic as studied in the Abbey. It's the style of religious art: the spiritual needs line-boundaries. He was wrong there: nobody can tell what stops another person's mind in its tracks. On the whole, in fact, softer paintings have the edge.

126

44 Dining with Isaiah

Is mysticism a trick of the brain or is it a genuine meeting with a reality outside the mind? Blake was so convinced of its reality that he sang with joy on his death bed. In *The Marriage of Heaven and Hell,* he had dinner with Isaiah and Ezekiel. 'Did God really speak to you?' he asked.

No,' replied Isaiah, 'I had mystic experiences.'

'Is that enough?' Blake went on.

'All poets think so,' Isaiah answered. 'At one time mystic experiences were common,' he added, 'though no longer.'

Locke rejected Plato's Ideas and Blake, in turn, rejected Locke because Locke couldn't see that the mystic vision is real, inborn and untaught. Things in the world may switch it on but it isn't of this world. Our reaction to beauty is likewise untaught and leads to a spiritual meeting place in the mind.

45 Yeats on Blake

Yeats is often called a mystic although I have my doubts: occultism, Golden Dawn Theosophy and Hermes Trismegistus are, like spiritualism, bogus. Yet Yeats had some perceptive things to say about a man who was a genuine mystic – William Blake.

In the early years of the 19th century, Yeats maintained, Blake had been ahead of his time. But now (now being 1897), in the dying years of Queen Victoria's reign, poets had caught up with him. In Blake's day, sermons fed souls, now poetry is the soul's food. Poetry is a divine revelation. Reason binds us to mortality but poetry is about beauty, and beauty is immortal.

46 Figures in a Mystic Landscape

Blake was almost a one-image artist – most of his work features the human figure, often unclothed. *Plate 38* in Blake's *Milton* shows two naked bodies, apparently both male, lying on a rock in the sea. An open-beaked bird with fully out-stretched wings hovers over them menacingly. The texture and contours of the rocks are perfectly etched. The inshore waves too are perfect – has anybody painted let alone etched waves so spiritually real (if not materially) as Blake could do? The far background, on the other hand, is disappointing. At first it looks like the sea with a scratched in horizon. On second thoughts, it's probably all sky.

The prone figures are Albion being cared for by Los, his creative side (Albion is each of us and also England). But it doesn't matter who they are: they're best looked on as humanity naked and exposed, beaten and fallen but about to rise again, in a wilderness of stone and sea. Having said that, what really makes it work is the rockscape and seascape. Without them the picture would lose most of its power.

Mystically speaking, landscape almost always works better than human figures, and soft outlines are better than hard ones (Blake believed the opposite). Landscape is what makes *Plate 70* of *Jerusalem* work. It's dominated by an enormous trilith (or triliton) which dwarves three female figures in Jane Austen frocks. A sun (or moon?) is seen – it can hardly be said to shine – between the uprights and the lintel of the great stone square arch. Once again, it's best to look at the picture divorced from the text (it must be something to do with Druids) and what you see is spiritual continuity through time.

47 Missing the Message

Trying to describe the mystic moment baldly in poetry or prose can sometimes work well enough to give a glimmering sense of what it's all about: painting it is another matter. Cecil Collins tried to do so by drawing angels, or spiritual messengers. Whatever stops thought is what works: painted angels ask for comment.

48 That Questionnaire

Laski's book, *Ecstasy*, hinged on a questionnaire. 'Do you know a sensation of transcendent ecstasy?' If the answer was 'yes', the follow-on questions were: 'How would you describe it?' 'What has induced it in you?' 'How many times in your life have you felt it – in units, tens, hundreds?' 'What is your religion or faith?' 'Do you know a feeling of creative inspiration?' 'Does it (inspiration, that is) seem to have anything in common with ecstasy?' 'What is your profession?'

It says a lot about her open-mindedness that she never had these experiences herself, although she was sometimes moved to near ecstasy by fabrics, ceramics and jewellery. All were craft items, all old, none was in use. New craft articles aren't triggers, she said, though that's not true: anything can be.

49 Mysticism and Business Skills

Mystic events are commonly graded on three levels. Laski follows this pattern, with the difference that she discovered them for herself via that questionnaire. Her top tier is the Unitive state (very rare and theologically suspect in monotheism). The bottom she called adamic after Adam and Eve the Garden of Eden. The middle rung is Knowledge because people who experience it learn something. Mostly they come away knowing (or, better, believing) that there's more to this world than the unaided ego can understand. This new knowledge doesn't usually boost your income, yet that's what is supposed to have happened to Bernard Berenson, the once famous authority on Renaissance Art (and who may also have been a bit of crook). Sometime in 1900, when he was in his mid-thirties, he was looking at the carved vegetation around the door of the church of S. Pietro near Spoleto in Italy. 'Suddenly stem, tendril and foliage became alive and, in becoming alive, made me feel as if I had emerged into the light after long groping in the darkness of an initiation. I felt as one illumined, and beheld a world where every outline, every edge, and every surface was in a living relation to me and not, as hitherto, in a merely cognitive one. Since that morning, nothing that is visible has been indifferent or even dull' (except, he added, for machine-made things). After that, he saw everything in its own radiance and vitality and, in

129

fact, felt no need of art at all because he was now his own artist with the gift of a great painter's sight.

He said of himself: 'For years, I had been inquiring. excavating, dredging my inner self, and searching in my conscious experience for a satisfying test' – a test, that is, by which to judge the quality of any given work of art. His mystical experience gave it to him. Laski said he'd been given the gift of a theory of aesthetics. It was also good for business which, in part, was matching Old Master paintings to Old Master painters. He didn't even have to be right: if dealers and buyers trusted him, he could make big money. Berenson was and did. He died rich.

50 Deus Aderit

On the lintel of his door in Switzerland Jung had carved, in a Latin translation from the Greek: *Vocatus atque non vocatus, deus aderit*: 'Invoked or uninvoked, a god is here'. A few people, by no means all it seems, have inside them a *deus* – or a realisation – which tells the ego that there's more to life than it can ever know. In middle age, as death gets nearer, this deus – called by Jung the Self – tries to break through the barrier between consciousness and the unconscious to get ego to behave. Only the Self knows how its own particular organism should live in order to become complete and therefore be in line with the laws of nature. By not listening to the Self, the ego inflicts a terrible penalty through a sense of loss and aimlessness, as well as hurting everybody around it.

51 A Job for Job

Some people interpret Blake's engraved illustrations for the *Book of Job* in a Jungian way. To them, Job is about the overcoming of ego by Self. Both Self and ego are levels of consciousness. Ego is the every day kind which sees the world only narrowly from its own point of view: Self sees the whole. In the end, Job's Self breaks through to his ego, wholeness is restored and the whole is thereby, and therefore, reconciled with God.

Iconoclasm, the word, was invented in the 18th century although it'd been a reality for at least a thousand years before then. In 726, icons throughout the Byzantine Empire were burned on the orders of Leo III who thought they were graven images. What his real motives were – if they were different other than the one given – I don't know if we know. What's certain is that this cast of mind crops up in every generation and is always equally destructive whatever the mindset which infects it.

A thousand years later, 17th century Puritans in England defiled churches by smashing stained glass, breaking statues, whitewashing paintings. Not that they always won. Failed iconoclasts fired muskets at the statue of the Madonna and Child in the niche above the High Street entrance to the University Church of St Mary the Virgin in Oxford. The holes are still there, so they say, along with the statue.

Patrixbourne in Kent was called Bourne – river – before the Patricks came over with the Conqueror. It's in *The Doomsday Book*. There were Saxon burials there and a church: pre-Norman stones make up some of the walls of the present St Mary's, the oldest part of which dates from around 1170. Five hundred years later Puritans (probably) vandalised the tympanum – animals and abstract patterns were left alone, only the religious figures were broken by hammers or musket butts. Christ in Majesty went, and the flanking angels, and the Lamb of God above the door. Archbishop Cranmer had had a summer palace nearby at Bekesbourne, in the same Nail valley, and it, too, was attacked by Puritans.

Oddly enough we may know the name of the ringleader – if, that is, he was also the man who broke the windows in nearby Canterbury Cathedral. The window breaker was General Sir Richard Culmer. He needed a ladder to bring the glass down but he seems to have had a way with words: 'rattling down proud Becket's glassy bones' was how he described what he'd done. Troops protected him while he did it, otherwise the people might have killed him. He was in his mid-forties at the time, and a priest of sorts, but a very unpopular one: when he was given the

131

living of Minster, his parishioners locked the church door against him and then offered him money to go away. It was the second church which refused to have him. When asked why he smashed Christ in the glass and not Satan, his answer was by now the familiar one – 'I was obeying orders, and they didn't include defying the Devil.' He died in Holland, where presumably he'd fled after the Restoration, at the age of seventy. Blue Dick, he was nicknamed – rather lamely given his record of vandalism and furious resentment because he refused to wear priestly black and wore only blue, a strange vanity for a such a zealot.

The iconoclast cast of mind is still with us, the mindset only has changed. Today it bans ideas which don't conform to its orthodoxy in science or schooling or how society should work. Great art, if not destroyed, is not encouraged – and, if Ruskin is right, that is an indictment of the health of the dominant mindset. In a hundred years the cast of mind will still be there though the mindset inhabiting it will be quite different – but still wanting to impose its ideas on what it hates. There's always something unhealthy about it. Perhaps it's just a literal, exoteric, mindset which is incapable of seeing anything esoteric in the world.

53 Hamlets, Hotspurs and Pickwicks

Only a minority of people, as we now know, have mystical experiences. The question which never seems to be asked, however, is this: are these events open to every kind of temperament, or just one? The assumption running through my earlier book, *Undertones*, is that they're mainly the province of introverts – because, by definition, it's a purely inner state and introverts, by their nature, live within their own minds. Aldous Huxley deals with the question in *The Perennial Philosophy*.

In it, he compares the teaching of *The Bhagavad-Gita* with William Sheldon's somatotypes. In *The Gita*, Krishna tells Arjuna about the three basic temperaments and their routes to salvation. Action-type people need to act but the trick is to do so without clinging to the ego. Personal devotion, also stripped of self, is the way to salvation for the second temperament.

Eliminating ego through contemplation is the proper method for the third. Huxley equates them with Sheldon's mesomorphs, endomorphs and ectomorphs. The mesomorph is the *Gita's* action man, the endomorph is the devotee, while the contemplative is the ectomorph.

More happily, Huxley also humanised them as Pickwicks, Hotspurs and Hamlets. Pickwick is the endomorph – the rotund, soft, extraverted food-lover whose life is centred around comfort, good company and his stomach. He's nostalgic for childhood, and needs other people when hurt.

Hotspur (mesomorph) is the big muscled action man, extraverted, lustful for power, a great disregarder of pain (his own and that of others). He stands for combat and competition. His nostalgia is for youth when the body works uncreakingly like a new machine. In trouble he needs action.

Hamlet is the lone ectomorphic introvert – a grotesquely oversensitive questioner and a great disliker of people. Hamlets don't care much about comfort, luxury or material things. When troubled, they need to be alone. They're over-evolved. Is theirs the temperament which recruits most mystics?

Theoretically, the answer must be 'no': stoppage of thought should be possible for all. All the same, it's hard to think of Hotspurs as anything other than exoteric Hirelings, while Marthas are more likely to be Pickwicks. In the West, we have no *secular* tradition of mysticism – historically, that's been left to cloistered monks and nuns, a natural life-choice for introverts but clearly not for the others.

The Sheldon-Huxley theory is a nice one but, of course, it fails when it touches reality. Few people are full-time Hamlets, Hotspurs or Pickwicks. Most are a mix of all three. What happens if no one temperament stands out because all are equal and equally diluted? Zen is more sophisticated. There's a *way*, or *do*, for practically everybody: *kado* for the poet, *gado* for the painter, *chado* for devotees of the Tea Ceremony, *bushido* for the soldier, *jindo* for the philosopher, *shodo* for the calligrapher, *kendo* and *judo* for fighters. (*Shinto* is the way of the gods.) Even so, I believe only something like one percent of the Japanese people are actively Zennist.

54 Eckhart and Orthodoxy

Roman Catholic mysticism, said Inge, is an 'imitation of Christ'. The Western mystic tried, that is, to re-live Christ's suffering. Orthodox mysticism, on the other hand, is about gaining the grace of the Holy Spirit and so being deified and changed internally into a different person, a different creature. Eckhart was this kind of mystic. Yet Eckhart could have known nothing about the Greek Church. His vision was his own.

55 Gottesfreunde

The church at the western end Christendom in the 14th century was corrupt. That, after all, is the theme of Langland's *Piers Plowman*: Chaucer's Pardoner is a pretty unsavoury character too.

In Germany, a loose group of lay and clerical mystics, called the Friends of God, took matters into their own hands: each of us has the right to set up an 'inner church' in corrupt or troubled times. All were followers of Eckhart and, like him, their epicentre was Strasbourg and Cologne but with a loose membership stretching from the Alps to the Low Country.

Johann Tauler was Strasbourg born and bred. Like all the Gottesfreunde, he spoke of a personal spirituality based on an innate divine spark: overcome the ego and let the Holy Spirit be your soul's teacher.

Like Eckhart, Tauler was a great preacher – all we know of him comes from surviving sermons and a single letter (all in German, not Medieval Latin). For him religion was entirely a matter of inward experience: no theologian can teach you anything about it. God's image is within: God chisels it out like a sculptor with a block of stone.

56 Tauler's Temple

Tauler likened people's minds to temples crowded with traders and money-changers (or thoughts and emotions) which have to be thrown out before you can grow spiritually. In a word – stop the mind's surging for a brief moment.

Eckhart, who simplified everything (no more ladders, scales, levels, rungs, stages from here to the Godhead) merely said you must rid yourself of ego and the tumult of your mind and you're there, automatically.

57 More on Marthas and Hirelings

Ruysbroeck, of course. wasn't the only one to recognise that what Alister Hardy called *The Something-More* isn't everybody's cup of tea. St Paul said that only the Perfect Man – that is, one who's mystically mature – is fully spiritual. (At least, that's Dean Inge's way of looking at what St Paul said.) Paul realised that a great many people are too earth-bound to know the spirit: the spiritual is understood only by people of judgement. It gives them 'life and peace'.

St Paul was a mystic: Origen, the Bishop of Caesarea who lived a hundred and fifty or so years later, was not. He separated people, after the manner perhaps of sheep and goats, into mystics and pistics, pneumatics and somatics, the esoteric and the exoteric.

Coleridge said everybody is either an Aristotelean or a Platonist. Inge put it yet another way: people are either mystics or Legalists, illuminated or traditional, Prophets or Priests (he was himself, quite literally, a priest and unmystical with it). William James noted this split also: his phrases were 'institutional' and 'personal religions'.

58 The Foot of the Ladder

There can be something very selfish (and therefore counter-counter-cosmic) in striving for the mystic experience if it's wanted only to escape the pain and misery of this world. It can become what St. Augustine called *fuga in solitudinem* – flight to solitude. Ruysbroeck said that when you've climbed the ladder to the top, you should come down again to help others. Eckhart thought Marthas are better than Marys because they're of more use to the world. St Teresa said people should be both. Underhill took her advice: she was a mystic in the morning, a director of spiritual retreats in the afternoon. To her mysticism was an experience with a practical outcome. Its chief ingredient was love.

59 Roast Pork and Eleusis

A few years ago, there was a story about how the Chinese invented roast pork: a house with a pig inside accidentally burned down. After that, roast pork became popular although it must have had an effect on house prices until somebody figured you didn't have burn the whole place down: a fire in a grate and a spit would do the trick.

I was reminded of the story while reading (in Karen Armstrong's *The Age of Transformation*) about the mysteries at Eleusis. Thousands of people massed, after two days without food, on the sea shore near Athens before marching to Eleusis, calling on Dionysius, the god of change, as they went. They reached the town at sunset and began winding by torchlight, lost and disorientated, through the streets before being herded into the blackness of a great unlit hall. There they watched, presumably in some kind of spot light, an animal sacrifice, following by something 'unspeakable', perhaps the acted out slaughter of a child. A play of some sort re-enacted Demeter's reunion with her daughter, Persephone, back from the dead for a brief season in the sun. (Inge had a slightly different version – people washed themselves spiritually clean in two salt-water lakes as well as in the sea. The sacramental food in the big shed was barley-meal, honey and water. An ear of corn (standing for Demeter) was what was revealed.)

By then the minds of the susceptible would have closed down, all thought stopped, allowing divine revelation to step inside the emptied mind. It was all a bit like burning the house down: there are easier ways of doing it, as Socrates told them.

Socrates used reason to defeat reason. Dialectics (like Zen *koans* and *mondos*) break the mind down into stillness and to an acceptance that it knows nothing, thus eliminating (for a time) ego. He stopped thought itself, step by step, through questions and non-answers, clearing away mental clutter and opening the mind to the spiritual. In *Laches*, for example, he asks what is bravery or courage? He'd been in action as a soldier in the Athenian army in the Peloponnesian War. Not that his lowly rank stopped him from reducing General Laches to intellectual impotence.

60 Who's Who in Dante

Being given a slot in *The Divine Comedy*, in the *Paradiso* at any rate, must have been a pretty cool accolade for pre-Dantean mystics. Unfortunately there was a long gap of around seven hundred years between the Patristic mystics and the ones of the Middle Ages. That gap, of course, was the Dark Ages when mystics, if not thin on the ground, were pretty much out of sight. St Augustine, of course, is high in the *Paradiso*. Dionysius the Areopagite is in *Canto X* – ten, that is, out of thirty. Cassian isn't in at all. St Paul is, as you'd expect.

Dante wrote in the early 14th century, only a hundred-odd years after the start of the Medieval wave of mystics. So the 12th century Scotsman, Richard of St Victor, was able to make it – into *Canto X* – grouped with Isadore and Bede, all three with 'glowing breath'.

Richard is singled out for his more than human mysticism. He should also be remembered for one of his similes. To reach the mystic moment you have to know yourself in order to strip out the ego. Getting to know yourself is like climbing a mountain: it's hard work but when you reach the peak you can see the far horizon on all sides. You see what a huge world you live in and how small you are.

The 12th century St Bernard of Clairvaux is much higher in the pecking order – *Canto XXX*. He briefly replaces Beatrice as Dante's guide when she returns to her own part of Heaven. St Bernard, Dante tells us, had known the peace of Paradise while still on earth. The poet, in fact, can't take his eyes off him: he compares himself to the kind of Croatian traveller who stares in amazement at the Veronica, the handkerchief imprinted with Christ's face. St Bernard has to re-direct Dante's eyes to the Virgin higher up in Heaven.

61 Sadness and Repose: Six Victorian Poems

Short pieces are the surest way to highlight the sadness and repose which mark out great art and make it a generator, at the very least, of undertones. As far as I know, only two of these six poets were mystics – Tennyson and Hopkins.

John Clare, a farm labourer, was briefly lionised (or patronised) as the Northamptonshire Peasant Poet in the 1820s and '30s. (He was born in 1793). He was a gifted man who'd been dealt a bad hand by fate – even the landscape on the edge of the Fens which meant so much to him was changed in his early lifetime by the Enclosure Acts. For his last twenty-three years he lived in the Northampton General Asylum for the insane, although he was free to roam the town and encouraged to write poetry. *I Am*, his most anguished verse, was written during this time. The House Steward copied his work into large books. If the fifth line of the first stanza seems a bit garbled, perhaps it's a scribal error? Clare died in 1864.

I am – yet what I am, none cares or knows;
My friends forsake me like a memory lost:
I am the self-consumer of my woes –
They rise and vanish in oblivions host,
Like shadows in love frenzied stifled throes
And yet I am, and live – like vapours tost
Into the nothingness of scorn and noise,
Into the living sea of waking dreams,
Where there is neither sense of life or joys,
But the vast shipwreck of my lifes esteems;
Even the dearest that I love best
Are strange – nay, rather, stranger than the rest.

I long for scenes where man hath never trod
A place where woman never smiled or wept
There to abide with my Creator God,
And sleep as I in childhood sweetly slept,
Untroubling and untroubled where I lie
The grass below, above, the vaulted sky.

Clare was sixteen when Tennyson was born in Lincolnshire,
north of the Fens. *Crossing the Bar* was written at the very end of
Tennyson's life, too. 'This crowns your life's work,' a friend said.
'Yes, it came to me in a moment.' That moment, it seems, came
in 1889 on a passage across the Solent to the Isle of Wight. He'd
been very ill, in fact had only three years to live. 'The Pilot has
been on board all the while,' he said, 'but in the dark I have not
seen him.' Tennyson asked his son, Hallam, to print the poem
as the end-piece in his collected works. It still is.

Sunset and evening star,
And one clear call for me!
And may there be no moaning of the bar,
When I put out to sea,

But such a tide as moving seems asleep,
Too full for sound and foam,
When that which drew from out the boundless deep
Turns again home.

Twilight and evening bell,
And after that the dark!
And may there be no sadness of farewell,
When I embark;

For tho' from out our bourne of Time and Place
The flood may bear me far,
I hope to see my Pilot face to face
When I have crost the bar.

Gerard Manley Hopkins was born in Chaucer's Stratford-
atte-Bowe in 1844, only three year after John Clare had been put   139
away in the Northampton Asylum. In his mature verses
Hopkins celebrates the landscape ('plotted and pieced – fold,

fallow, and plough') created by the Enclosure Acts which so distressed Clare. But the first draft of *Heaven-Haven* was written when he was still only twenty (in 1864, the year of Clare's death) and before he'd developed his own very distinctive style. He was still at Oxford, still an Anglican, but already thinking of a converting to Catholicism and a religious life. The poem seems to be more about a personal longing for peace than about a nun taking her last vows, as its subtitle (*a nun takes the veil*) suggests

> I have desired to go
> Where springs not fail,
> To fields where flies no sharp and sided hail
> And a few lilies blow.
>
> And I have asked to be
> Where no storms come,
> Where the green swell is in the havens dumb,
> And out of the swing of the sea.

Robert Louis Stevenson (born 1850) is best known now for *The Strange Case of Dr Jekyll and Mr Hyde* and *Treasure Island*. Remember Long John Silver, the Benbow Inn, and Blind Pugh bearing The Black Spot to Billy Bones? And Cap'n Flint dying in Savannah, calling for rum? Or Ben Gunn, the castaway, longing for a 'little bit of Christian cheese' (toasted, preferably)? The names are undertones in themselves.

Stevenson's short poem, *Requiem*, used to be equally well known. He'd been a sickly child and never had good health as a man. Perhaps a weariness shows in the poem which he wrote when he was still only in his thirties and which is inscribed, I believe, on his gravestone in Samoa where he died in 1894.

> Under the wide and starry sky,
> Dig the grave and let me lie.
> Glad did I live and gladly die,
> And I laid me down with a will.
> This be the verse you grave for me:
> Here he lies where he longed to be;
> Home is the sailor, home from sea,
> And the hunter home from the hill.

A E Housman spent much of his life correcting corruption, putting right what had gone wrong, returning, in his own small way, chaos to cosmos, although some people think he wasted his life correcting scribal errors in the work of an obscure Latin poet, Manilius. *The Land of Lost Content* is untitled (it is just *XL*) in *A Shropshire Lad* where it was first published in 1896. Laski, as we've seen, thought he was a mystic, though that's far from clear. All the same his English poetry had the right mix of sadness and repose:

> Into my heart an air that kills
> From yon far country blows:
> What are those blue remembered hills,
> What spires, what farms are those?
>
> That is the land of lost content,
> I see it shining plain,
> The happy highways where I went
> And cannot come again.

Wilfred Owen, finally, was born in 1893, exactly a century after John Clare. If Clare grew into a Victorian, Owen was growing into a 20th century man when he died in the last Victorian conflict of them all, the Great War. He wrote *Anthem for Doomed Youth* in a hospital for shell-shocked soldiers. Yet Owen was also doomed: he was killed by machine gun fire leading a platoon of the Manchester Regiment across a canal a few days before the War ended. The old custom of drawing the curtains, or pulling down the blinds, to mark a death in the house has now ended.

> What passing-bells for these who die as cattle?
> Only the monstrous anger of the guns.
> Only the stuttering rifles' rapid rattle
> Can patter out their hasty orisons.
> No mockeries now for them; no prayers nor bells;
> Nor any voice of mourning save the choirs,
> The shrill, demented choirs of wailing shells;
> And bugles calling for them from sad shires.
> What candles may be held to speed them all?

Not in the hands of boys, but in their eyes
Shall shine the holy glimmers of good-byes.
The pallor of girls' brows shall be their pall;
Their flowers the tenderness of patient minds,
And each slow dusk a drawing-down of blinds.

62 Hollow Men

T S Eliot wanted mystical experiences but never had any, at least not if we take the *Four Quartets* to be autobiographically accurate.

The Hollow Men was originally part of a longer work which, when cut down to size by Ezra Pound, became *The Wasteland*. The hollowmen exist in a kingdom even less vital and more desolate than that. Yet the poem does have undertones. Take these two lines for example:

... there, the eyes are
Sunlight on a broken column.

That's more like a haiku-image, the man-made and the natural side by side, both imbued with a sense of stillness and sadness. Is it possible that a poet like Eliot can pass a low level adamic experience on to others and yet not feel it himself? So it seems.

63 Shadows of Eternity

For an explicit example of an undertone at work you could do worse then read Henry Vaughan's poem *The Retreate*. Vaughan lived most of his life by the River Usk in Brecknockshire. He'd been a soldier in the King's cause in the Civil War, otherwise he lived the quiet live of a country doctor, dying at the age of seventy-three in 1695. George Herbert influenced his poetry.

Today he's best known for the mystic lines 'I saw Eternity the other night,/Like a great ring of pure and endless light'. In *The Retreate* the mysticism is less overt, subtle enough to be an undertone in fact. The extreme mysticism of early childhood has gone, but all is not lost. In the poem, he's looking back to late boyhood 'When ...

> ... on some gilded Cloud or Flowere
> My gazing soul would Swell and houre,
> And in those weaker glories spy,
> Some shadows of eternity'.

Those 'shadows of eternity' are extrovertive, adamic undertones.

64 Undertones and the Poetry of Poverty

George Crabbe (1754-1832) was the poet of rural reality. He's best remembered for the Peter Grimes story which Benjamin Britten made into an opera called – not unnaturally – *Peter Grimes*. The story's told in Crabbe's long poem, *The Borough* which in reality is Aldeburgh in Suffolk:

> No: cast by Fortune on a frowning coast,
> Which neither groves nor happy valleys boast
> I paint the Cot
> As truth will paint it, and as the Bards will not.

Crabbe's father was a taxman and he himself became a doctor and then a clergyman: for a time he was chaplain to the Duke of Rutland before being given the living of Trowbridge in Wiltshire. Edmund Burke himself helped him get his early poetry published. (Crabbe was also an amateur entomologist, an expert on beetles.)

Peter Grimes, a fisherman, is a bad lot who beat and abused his father and then caused the deaths of three orphan boys who've been taken from London workhouses and bound apprentice to him. In the end he is forbidden to take on boys and must hire free men, though none will work for him. He fails to prosper and skulks in his boat in the lonely reaches of the local river until the ghost of his dead father and two of the boys return to walk on the water and haunt him. In the end he runs away and dies, in terror of Hell, in a distant parish workhouse.

Crabbe was almost an exact contemporary of William Blake

(three years older, in fact). Unlike Blake, he was a conventional Augustan poet of the heroic couplet and his verse reads as easily as prose. All this sounds unpromising from an undertone or mildly mystical point of view – rural poverty, harsh reality conveyed in the repeated beat of iambic pentameter couplets? Yet if we take as an example the Peter Grimes section of *The Borough* we find two things which create undertones. To begin with, the character and actions of Grimes himself adds something to the mind. As does, secondly, the imagery of the coastal and river landscape where the poem is set. There's stillness here and sadness of the pitying kind. But there's also, in some places, a sadness for things. Here is a passage from the Peter Grimes section of *The Borough* which make those last points plainer. Grimes, shunned by the village, lurks on the river:

> Thus by himself compelled to live each day,
> To wait for certain hours the tide's delay;
> At the same times the same dull views to see,
> The bounding marshbank and the blighted tree;
> The water only, when the tides were high,
> When low, the mud half-covered and half-dry;
> The sunburnt tar that blisters on the planks,
> And bankside stakes in their uneven ranks;
> Heaps of entangled weeds that slowly float,
> As the tide rolls by th' impeded boat.
> When tides were neap, and, in the sultry day,
> Through the tall bounding mudbanks made their way,
> Which on each side rose swelling, and below
> The dark warm flood ran silently and slow;
> There anchoring, Peter chose from man to hide,
> There hang his head, and view the lazy tide
> In its hot slimy channel slowly glide;
> Where the small eels that left the deeper way
> For the warm shore, within the shallows play;
> Where gaping mussels, left upon the mud,
> Slope their slow passage to the fallen flood;
> Here dull and hopeless he'd lie down and trace
> How sidelong crabs had scrawled their crooked race;

Or sadly listen to the tuneless cry
Of fishing gull or clanging goldeneye.

65 Spirituality and the Poet Robert Nichols

Robert Nichols (1893-1944) can be added to the lengthening list of Victorian writers who were also mystics. He's little known these day, even as a War Poet although his name is on the stone in Westminster Abbey commemorating them.

In the Great War he served with the Royal Artillery on the Somme. He begins his poem, *At the Wars*, by asking what comes most immediately to mind now there is no certainty of another tomorrow? Not the voices of friends, not the eyes of a lover, but England as expressed in her countryside.

An upland field when spring's begun,
Mellow beneath the evening sun?....

Paths that lead a shelving course
Between the chalk scarp and the gorse.

... now a lane
Glitters with warmth of May-time rain.
And on a shooting briar I see
A yellow bird who sings to me.

But Laski also uses Nichols to show how ecstasy and inspiration are one and the same. One dawn, Nichols stood alone on the bow of a steamer sailing over a slight swell into a rising sun. He felt a 'central excitement surrounded by ... deep, tranquil and joyful satisfaction'. Light glinted off the sea in long cursive lines like Arabic writing. The sun is writing a poem on the sea, he thought. Strangely, it brought to mind a post-card with a picture of a poet, possibly Persian, he'd once bought in the British Museum. A new line of poetry slipped unasked into his mind: 'The sun an ancient, serene poet'.

For many people today art is left-wing politics in another guise. For others it's about dissecting human nature. For almost nobody is it spiritual: spiritual, that is, in the sense of triggering off a mystical experience, generating undertones, or just circling around the divine exoterically. We have, in fact, reached a point where even Professors of English in major universities think that Wordsworth was just a poet of childhood.

Ruskin believed art is a touchstone by which we can judge the health of a society. What is deep inside people shows up in their art. If their art is brutal, degraded, ugly or empty, so will they be. Good art is spiritual in the esoteric sense. Blake agreed: degraded art degrades society – and a degraded society, he might have added, degrades art in a positive feedback loop (a phrase from cybernetics not then invented):

> Degrade first the arts if you'd mankind degrade,
> Hire idiots to paint with cold light and hot shade.

All that matters with any work of art is what it does for you. It has to expand the mind either by closing down thought, by adding a new mental landscape, or by leaving permanent undertones or illumination behind. In the end, perhaps, generating undertones is the most important thing it can do. You may forget the details of Greek myths but the sunlight they convey will alway stay with you as lifelong undertones: you may not remember who said what in *Alice in Wonderland* or may have been dismayed by the shallowness of the plots in Sherlock Holmes but the undertones of Carroll's strange world and Conan Doyle's Victorian London will be always be there.

Ruskin was also, I think, the first to notice that feelings of sadness and repose lie at the heart of all great painting (they are in fact what make it great). They are, I suppose, moods but neither English nor Latin has a word for them, only phrases: *lachrymae rerum* and 'tears for things'. More subtly, Japanese has, I believe, four words for four moods: *sabi, wabi, aware, jugen. Sabi* is sadness for the loneliness of things. *Jugen* for the strangeness that things should exist. *Aware* for the brevity of the

146

life of things, of passingness. *Wabi* is a sense of greatness, perhaps more awe than sadness.

To experience these things you need *miyabi* (sensitivity to delicate degrees of beauty) and *fuga* (sensitivity to the four moods) – or at least so R H Blyth informs us. The lack of them, perhaps, goes some way to explaining Hirelings who are, in other words, people with something missing from their make up.

Sadness and repose, of course, can't be consciously conjured up: they come through inspiration – the breath of the gods – which is also a lesser kind of mysticism. Because of this, great art is rare. Great poetry, perhaps, is the rarest of them all: since Chaucer, I don't suppose more than three or four hundred great lines have been written in English. (Verse is common and, nowadays, prose non-verse even more so.) Along with repose and sadness, poetry has to be memorable, slipping easily into the mind and memory and staying there. Poetry is quotable. You can quote it to make a point.

Ruskin thought that beauty is part of something higher, and therefore able to impart the spiritual. Inge would have agreed. To him, in fact, Reality is 'a Kingdom of Values': Goodness, Truth and Beauty. If there's no beauty in us, we can't see Beauty and are therefore banned from Eternity. This, said Inge, is the central principle of mysticism.

Inge also had a bit to say about symbols which he saw as connectors between time and eternity. 'A symbol is a revelation of the Inscrutable,' he quotes Goethe as saying. He also quotes St Paul and Plato who said we dimly see the Invisible though the visible. Symbols represent 'the infinite in the finite'.

Symmetry is needed too. All poetry has to be a pattern of sound based on a language's deepest characteristic. In Japanese, that's length of syllables. Poetry in English, on the contrary, is a steady pattern of stressed and unstressed syllables. It's always been that way – which tells us just how fundamental it is. In Old English we have:

Thaes ofereode   thisses swa maeg
(That over-went   this so may:
That calamity passed and so may this one.)

And in Middle English:

> In a summer season   when soft was the sun

Stressed syllables alone hold both of them together. That's all that Hopkins was saying with his Sprung Rhythm. Take care of the stressed syllables and the unstressed can take care of themselves. Ballads do. So do nursery rhymes. Once you've memorised *Humpty Dumpty,* you've mastered English prosody.

But poetry also works spiritually in a mechanical way. The mystic moment is revealed when thought is stopped by something, and poetry can be that something which stops it. It shocks the mind in two ways. First through images carried into the mind by words, in which case the words are less important than the image – they're just carriers. The second way is through the sound of syllables chiming, echoing, rhyming and combining, rather like music. For poets like Swinburne, sound is all that matters. Provence, to him, was less a place, more a euphony:

> By a tideless dolorous midland sea
> In a land of sand and ruin and gold.

For the carriage of images, on the other hand, nobody has yet beaten the Japanese haiku. They work even in translation simply because what they convey is so concrete. All the same, as Basho said, they need to have – and need to convey – grace, mystery, tranquillity and elegance. Blyth went further: a haiku is a sacrament in its own right. It's spiritual poetry perfected, purpose-built for creating undertones by thought-blocking. And it does so mainly through concrete images. This is a paraphrase, for example, of a Blyth translation of a haiku by Basho:

> The tolling of the evening bronze
> Bell fades,
> A scent of flowers rises.

It'll be a temple bell, struck by a swung baulk of timber like a battering ram. That imagery might work but, for an English setting, it could just as easily be the last slow tolling of a solitary bell after all the changes have been rung on all the bronze bells in the belfry. You're in a garden with highly scented flowers in a warm, long twilight at the end of a hot day in June. And it's a long time ago: today won't do.

The trick is to let the imagery under-mine the over-mind. Let it smother thinking as it would (more easily) if you stood there in the evening light as the tone of the bell vibrated into silence and the scent of the flowers rose to fill the sound-vacated space. That time and that place have been preserved and made portable in a simple poem. It should peel open something in your mind to let you experience a sense of the eternal.

Need the words make sense? On the whole, yes, if only because, when confronted with a puzzle, the mind usually won't rest until it's solved – and rest, of course, is part of how art works: large parts of Eliot to this day are marred by obscurity and therefore work only intermittently.

Form and content, then, are both important. On the other hand, poetry which is about an emptiness at the heart of things may not work at all, or at least not work well. The emptiness of Larkin's *Mr Bleaney,* about a man dying alone in a rented room, shrinks the soul. It should enlarge it. These do:

> Vacant shuttles weave the wind.
> (T S Eliot)

> Time held me green and dying
> Though I sang in my chains like the sea.
> (Dylan Thomas)

> And therefore I have sailed the seas and come
> To the holy city of Byzantium
> (W B Yeats)

Sadness, repose, symbols, symmetry, capital-B Beauty are all there. All are now old.

67 Human Newts

Inge was a Platonist – a Christian one but a Platonist nevertheless: he seemed to agree with St Augustine who said that the Incarnation was the only doctrine he didn't find in Plato, and that was why he became a Christian. The Platonist, Inge declared, loves all that's lovely and beautiful because these things come from our home in a far country and we must head there, always. Sin is from ignorance, a narrowness of understanding. We sense the Invisible through the visible. We're like amphibians in that we can live in two worlds – the 'ponderable' which is here and now, and the 'imponderable' which is one of beauty, goodness and truth. The Eternal is internal and so we straddle the border between the material and the spiritual. We should live in both, but the West has chosen, almost exclusively, the exoteric and the material.

68 Afterword

A major mystic event can change people forever. The best example is the Buddha. For forty years he'd looked for enlightenment: for forty years he shared what he found. He lived simultaneously in this cosmos and the counter-cosmos of his mind. That's unusual: more usually – but still unusually – the counter-cosmos leaves something behind which drives people on to a new way of living. Wesley had his moment one night in Aldersgate Street near the old Roman wall in London and, then, perhaps without ever experiencing it again, spent the rest of his life preaching.

For most lesser people, the counter-cosmos balloons (or, more likely, forms a small bubble) only briefly and leaves no lasting change behind when it collapses. Experiencing this small-scale adamic event, in other words, is all very well but can it be used to change a life's direction? Without, that is, becoming preachy or pious? What would it be like to live, if not totally rid of ego, at least not ego-ridden, and always aware of the background radiation of eternity?

Appendix

Sir Alister Clavering Hardy, who was born in Nottingham in 1896, had mystical experiences as a schoolboy in Oundle although he kept them to himself throughout his working life. When he retired, at the age of seventy-three in 1969, he set up his Religious Experience Unit in Manchester College, Oxford. (Now it's the Alister Hardy Research Centre in the University of Wales, Lampeter.)

By working life, I mean a very distinguished career as a zoologist and marine biologist. He was successively a professor of zoology at the universities of Hull, Aberdeen and Oxford. In his late thirties he'd sailed in the Royal Research Ship *Discovery* (Scott's and Shackleton's originally) to study whales in the South Seas. On the voyage, between 1925 and '27, he invented a device for collecting and preserving unbroken streams of plankton. The Plymouth-based Sir Alister Hardy Foundation for Ocean Science, the first of his legacies, has carried on doing so continuously since 1931.

In 1940, he was made a Fellow of the Royal Society. In 1957, he was knighted. In the Great War he'd been a Captain in the Northern Cyclist Battalion, a home defence unit which never went to France. He was at Exeter College, Oxford, when war broke out. His last book, *Darwin and the Spirit of Man,* was published in 1984 when he was eighty-eight. He died the following year.

On top of all that, Hardy was a good amateur watercolourist. Some of his paintings are, of course, of sea life but others are of the island of South Georgia, the Cotswolds, and a series of temples and spiritual places in Japan, China and Burma. They are, I think, full of mystical sensitivity, the South Georgia landscapes in particular. Books of some of his paintings have been printed: the main collection is with the University of Wales, Lampeter.

Aldous Huxley was born in 1894 in Godalming in the

Stockbroker Belt of Surrey (H G Wells territory in *War of the Worlds* and other science fiction novels) and was extremely well connected: his grandfather was the Huxley who defended Darwin against Soapy Sam Wilberforce, Bishop of Oxford. His father was a schoolmaster at Charterhouse, editor of *The Cornhill Magazine,* and a biographer (mainly of his own father). Aldous was also the great-nephew of Matthew Arnold and nephew of Mrs Ward, the novelist. Two brothers were biologists. (Another committed suicide.) He was also an old Etonian (he taught French there, for a short time, to George Orwell among others) and a Balliol man.

His was of the Great War generation but he didn't serve because of poor eyesight: for a time he'd been nearly blind through inflammation of his corneas. His sight always seems to have troubled him though his second wife, whom he married in 1956, said he was perfectly cured. He tried the Bates Method and wrote approvingly about it in *The Art of Seeing,* published in the early years of the Second World War.

Meanwhile, back during the Great War, he'd worked as a farm labourer at Garsington, the Oxfordshire retreat of Ottoline Morrell and the Bloomsbury set. Huxley satirised them his early Post-War novel, *Crome Yellow.* All the same, he met his first wife there, a Belgian woman. Post-War they lived in Italy (close to D H Lawrence) and it was there, in his late thirties, that he wrote *Brave New World,* the one book for which he's probably now best known.

In 1937 he moved to California with his family. US citizenship was denied him because he refused to swear he'd take up arms in the country's defence: he was a philosophical, not a religious, pacifist. In California he made a friend of Kristnamurti and became involved with Vedanta. (In fact it seems to have been through Huxley that his fellow English exile, Christopher Isherwood, became a disciple of Swami Prabhavananda. Huxley wrote the preface to Isherwood's translation of *The Bhagavad Gita.*) One result of all of this was *The Perennial Philosophy,* an overview of mysticism illustrated with brief quotations from most of the world's esoteric traditions.

He tried his hand at Hollywood movie scripts but was not

good at popular stuff. In 1955, he undertook the experiment with mescalin which he wrote about in *The Doors of Perception*. He died, aged sixty-nine, of cancer of the throat, within two hours of Kennedy's assassination in 1963 and on the same day as C S Lewis.

Huxley was not a mystic. His brother called him an overview man, a universalist (or generalist). Even his novels are about ideas. In temperament and physique he closely matched the cerebrotonic/ectomorph of William Sheldon's somatotypes. (Huxley knew Sheldon, too.)

William Ralph Inge died aged ninety-four in 1954 and was therefore a mid-Victorian by birth (he was born in Crayke in the North Riding where his father was the curate). He was taught at home before going to Eton and then King's College, Cambridge, prize-winning and over-working all the way. Depression and deafness marred his life – worsening deafness for all of it, depression until he married at the age of forty-five. He was ordained fairly late – aged thirty-two – probably because he needed to find a 'sound intellectual basis' for belief. Hence, of course, his interest in mysticism. Plotinus and Platonism were life long passions, and mysticism (although he seems *not* to have been a mystic himself) fascinated him to the end: his last book, published when he was eight-eight, was *Mysticism in Religion*.

He was thirty-eight when he gave the Bampton Lectures, in Oxford, which were printed in 1899 as *Christian Mysticism*. Mysticism he considered to be concentrated religion, religion boiled down to its essence. He held the Lady Margaret Chair of Philosophy in Cambridge for four years before unexpectedly becoming, in 1911, Dean of St Paul's. At first it wasn't a happy appointment – the Chapter were theologically reactionary: Inge was a liberal. Politically, on the other hand, he was a bit of a reactionary (or a realist) himself: he was called the Gloomy Dean because of his opinions about the folly of democracy, the inanity of progress and the grievous state of society. For twenty-five years, until 1946, he wrote a weekly column about these things in the London *Evening Standard* and so was well known outside the church. He worried that Western civilisation was finished: it

153

could be saved only by a new spiritual religion – a blending of New Testament Christianity and the esotericism of Neoplatonism.

He's said to have been a fine preacher who drew the crowds. Oddly, too, he was an animal rights advocate: if the animal kingdom had a religion, he said, mankind would be its Satan. He left the Deanery at the age of seventy-four but only to carry on writing in retirement in Oxfordshire. His wife died five years before him.

William James held Chairs of Psychology *and* Philosophy at Harvard. He was a member of the university's Metaphysical Club in the 1870s when Peirce outlined the basic idea behind Pragmatism, the All-American philosophy. Later James added his own version, Radical Empiricism. His ideas about 'the stream of consciousness' influenced the 20th century's *avant garde* and modernism. He set up one of the first psychology laboratories in America, while his two volume *The Principles of Psychology* (1890) was a standard textbook for many years. He's credited with being the founder of functionalism and inspiring Skinner's Behaviourism.

Both in Pragmatism and in his own Radical Empiricism there's an emphasis on practicality and outcome. Additionally, running through James's thought is the idea of singleness, oneness, wholeness. Mind/body, for example, are a single whole – grief and weeping, therefore, can't be separated from that inherent unity: we grieve because we cry, we cry because we grieve. As James put it: 'We feel sorry because we cry, angry because we strike.' (This is called the James-Lange theory because the Danish psychologist, Carl Lange, thought of it at the same time, and independently.)

As a boy James travelled widely in France and Germany with his family, who were independently wealthy. (His father was a Swedenborgian: mysticism was in the family from his birth in New York in 1842). He was trilingual in English, French and German. As a youth he wanted to be a painter and studied art for a year before switching to chemistry in Harvard before switching to medicine in the same university from where, still restless and still a student, he joined a scientific expedition to the

Amazon: 'I was, body and soul, in a more indescribably hopeless, homeless and friendless state than I ever want to be in again.' Back home again, his health ruined, he suffered from depression. He broke off his studies to go to Germany for a time. There he met Hermann von Helmholtz who was already famous as the inventor of the ophthalmoscope and for his work on tones and overtones (James himself was tone deaf). Back in Harvard, James graduated as a medical doctor in 1869 at the age of twenty-seven.

In the 1890s he embarked on his original, never-before-done work on the psychology of religion. His findings were first made public in the 1901/2 Gifford lectures in Edinburgh. These, slightly revised, were printed as *The Varieties of Religious Experience*. The book has a subtitle: *A Study in Human Nature*. It is not, therefore, wholly about mysticism but also deals with other ways in which people relate to Divinity, with sections on religion and healthy-mindedness, religion and sickness of soul, the split self, and even saintliness. Apart from case studies, he – or his researchers – read diaries and autobiographies from around the world.

His early psychological ideas are now out-dated, though he's acknowledged as a founder of the discipline. Pragmatism, particularly his own Radical Empiricism, was revived in the 1960s. His work on mysticism, on the other hand, was seminal in the scientific West and he's recognised, I believe, as one of the founding minds behind Transpersonal Psychology. He died of a heart problem in 1910, aged sixty-eight, at home in New Hampshire. Henry James, the novelist, was his younger brother. Neither married. Two other brothers were killed in the American Civil War.

Marghanita Laski was born in Manchester in 1915 and died in London seventy-two years later, in 1988. During that time she'd been a journalist, a novelist and is said to have been the most prolific contributor to the Oxford English Dictionary of them all – a quarter of a million slips. She also persuaded the editor to use non-literary quotes and revise the First Edition (how can you do that?). For several years, also, she was a TV panellist, appearing in *The Brains Trust* in the 1950s, *What's My Line* ('50s into the '60s), and *Any Questions* also in the 1960s.

Little Boy Lost (1949) is a tear-jerker of a novel about a child in a French orphanage. He'd been taken there after his mother had died in wartime France. Post-War, the dead woman's widower goes there to find his son. Is this boy theirs? Four years later, in 1953, she published *The Victorian Chaise-longue*. The idea came from Arthur Mee's *One Thousand Beautiful Things*. Mee tells the story of a monk who goes for a walk in the fields to listen to a lark. Something strange then happens. Back in his monastery nobody knows him, he knows nobody: in those few brief moments of ecstasy, a hundred years had passed. *The Victorian Chaise-longue* is about a woman who is sent back through time into the body of her *alter ego*. As fiction it worked: nobody said it was stupid. But why was it so readily accepted? Was time really an illusion as some ecstatics – her word for mystics – claimed? This was one of reasons for her private study of mysticism. *Ecstasy,* her book about her findings, was published in 1961.

Caroline Spurgeon was born in India in 1869. Her mother died giving birth to her, while her father – an officer in the Herefordshire Regiment – died only five years later. She was educated at Cheltenham Ladies' College and London University from where she went on to an academic career, eventually becoming Professor of English in Bedford College, London, in 1913. That same year she published *Mysticism and English Literature,* an original work since, as far as I know, nobody before her had realised how many English writers were mystics. She asked: 'what does the mystic see?' and replied: 'Unity underlying diversity.' She was not herself a mystic.

In 1918 she went to the United States with the British Educational Mission. There she met Virginia Gildersleeve, an academic at Columbia University. After that, they spent every summer together until Professor Spurgeon's death in 1942. That was in Tucson, Arizona, where she'd gone in 1936 because the climate eased the pain of her arthritis. She's best known for a study of Shakespeare's imagery.

Walter Terence Stace was born a High Victorian in London in 1886 and died at Laguna Beach, California, eighty-one years later. From Fettes he went to Trinity, Dublin where he read philosophy. By then he seems to have had some kind of religious conversion and planned to become an Anglican priest. His family had other ideas and in 1910 the Colonial Office posted him to Ceylon, as Sri Lanka was then called. In his twenty years there he rose to be a magistrate or judge, I think, as well as mayor of Colombo. He thus missed the Great War. Instead, in the cool of each tropical morning, he wrote books on philosophy – well enough to get him asked, in 1932, to Princeton University. There, three years later, he was appointed Stuart Professor of Philosophy, and there he stayed until his retirement in 1955. Although an authority on Hegel, he was himself, unremarkably, an empiricist in the English-speaking tradition. More remarkably, in his mid-seventies he wrote two of the standard works on mysticism: *The Teachings of the Mystics* and *Mysticism and Philosophy* were published in the US in the same year, 1960. Both have long been out of print, which tells us a bit about the state of the spiritual in the present day West. He wasn't a mystic.

Evelyn Underhill (born in 1875 in Wolverhampton) read history *and* botany at King's College for Women, in London. She was also, variously, a yachtswoman, bookbinder, novelist, cat lover, poet, designer of wood and metal art work, and a 'director of souls'. For several summers in the late 19th and early 20th century she travelled in Italy and France, a cultural tourist. She was thirty-four when she married Hubert Moore, a barrister (as was her father: her mother was the daughter of a JP). The year of her marriage was also the year when she finally converted to Christianity. In 1911 she wrote the book, *Mysticism*, for which she's now largely still known. It was through this book, too, that she met Baron Friedrich von Hügel who became her spiritual mentor until his death in 1925. (*Mystics in the Church* came out in that same year.) As a Christian, she followed St Teresa's advice to combine Mary/ Martha. As a married woman, she was able to write in the mornings and visit the poor and 'direct souls' in the afternoons. She became an Anglican only when she was forty-eight in 1921, and was from then on well known as a director of spiritual retreats. In the First World War she worked for Naval Intelligence: in the Second she was a pacifist.

Her novels (*The Grey World* (1904), *The Lost World* (1907), *The Column of Dust* (1909)), are about the need to live in the twin worlds of the physical and the spiritual. Judging by her books, she was probably an extrovertive mystic in Stace's sense: this world is transfigured, brightened and made holy by the divine. But to her mysticism had to be practical – it meant working in the world, not succumbing to holy joy and absenting yourself. To live fully, people need to free themselves of ego.

Selected Bibliography

Armstrong, Karen *The Great Transformation: the World in the Time of Buddha, Socrates, Confucius and Jeremiah,* Atlantic Books, London, 2006

Blyth, R H *Zen in English Literature and Oriental Classics,* The Hokuseido Press, Tokyo, 1942

Ferguson, John *An Illustrated Encyclopaedia of Mysticism and the Mystery Religions,* Thames and Hudson, London, 1976

Hardy, Sir Alister *The Spiritual Nature of Man,* Clarendon Press, Oxford, 1979

Huxley, Aldous *The Perennial Philosophy,* Chatto and Windus, London, 1980

Inge, William Ralph *Christian Mysticism,* Methuen, London, 1899

Inge, William Ralph *Mysticism in Religion,* Rider & Company, London, 1969

James, William *The Varieties of Religious Experience,* Penguin, London, 1985

Laski, Marghanita *Ecstasy in Secular and Religious Experiences,* Jeremy P Tarcher, Los Angeles, 1976

Polkinghorne, Sir John *Science and Theology,* SPCK, London, 1998

Spurgeon, Caroline F E *Mysticism and English Literature.* Cambridge University Press, Cambridge, 1913.

Stace, Walter Terence *The Teachings of the Mystics,* Mentor, New York, 1960

Stace, Walter Terence *Mysticism and Philosophy,* Macmillan, London, 1961

Stannard, Russell (ed.) *God for the 21st Century,* SPCK, London, 2000

Sullivan, Dick *Undertones: Mild Mysticism in an Age of Umber,* Coracle Books, Thornham Magna, 2010

Sullivan, Dick *Counter-Cosmos: the Mind of the Mystic,* Coracle Books, Thornham Magna, 2011

Suzuki, D T *An Introduction to Zen Buddhism*, ed. Christmas Humphreys, Foreword C G Jung, Hutchinson, London,

Underhill, Evelyn *Mystics of the Church,* James Clarke. London, 1975

Underhill, Evelyn *Mysticism,* Wipf and Stock, Eugene, Oregon, 2002

Index

161

162